I do or I don't

Cultivating a Godly Marriage in Today's World

John Lehman

Endorsements

In *I Do or I Don't*, Dr. Lehman provides an insightful
and practical resource for church leaders and couples
alike. Readers will sense John's gracious spirit as
he encourages couples to strengthen their marriage
for the glory of God using time-tested, biblical
principles. John's expertise flows, not just from
years of counseling and pastoring and conference-
speaking, but from leading a marriage that really
works! Struggling couples should take heart ... and
take notes!

Brad Stille, Pastor of First Baptist Church of Wixom, MI

Gospel truth and biblical principles—this book will
take both and bring them to bear on marriage. The
Scripture is full of truth that will guide and direct our
marriages. So, whether you are soon to be married or
have been for years—read, meditate on, and apply the
truths in this book.

Jeremy McMorris, Lead Pastor, Liberty Baptist Church, Dalhart, TX

In an age when marriage books guide couples with
man-centered, self-help principles and ideas, *I Do or I
Don't* is a refreshing resource for couples who desire
a Christ-centered, Spirit-empowered marriage. John's
book lays out the essentials of a godly marriage
in an approach that is straightforward, easy to

read, practical, and above all biblical. The teaching found within this book has personally impacted my marriage and has equipped me to counsel other couples. Thank you for this blessed resource!

Ben Ice, Family Life Ministries, Calvary Baptist Church, Simpsonville, SC

Every day is really a choice of I Do or I Don't. I Do or I Don't want to be humble. I Do or I Don't want to be kind. I Do or I Don't want to be patient. I Do or I Don't want to be selfless. I Do or I Don't want to be compassionate. I Do or I Don't want to love like Christ loved the Church. I Do or I Don't want to submit as unto the Lord. This books lays out a "how to" in following biblical guidelines and "how to" be that spouse who says, "I Do want to love as Christ loved the church in very practical terms." I have lived alongside this man for thirty-three years and he has proven his faithfulness over and over again to me. Because he "practices what he preaches," I Do encourage you to consider utilizing this book for your own personal edification and your own marriage enrichment, as well as assisting others in their pursuit of God's will for their lives in the portrayal of Christ and the Church.

Suzie Lehman, John's wife

I Do or I Don't
Cultivating a Godly Marriage in Today's World

This (paperback) edition: 978-0-9899532-6-9

Hardcover edition: 978-0-9899532-5-2

ePub: 978-0-9899532-7-6

MOBI: 978-0-9899532-8-3

Typeset by Caroline McCausland (www.greatpublishing.org)

Published by www.greatwriting.org, Greenville, South Carolina
info@greatwriting.org

Cover design by www.greatwriting.org

Printed in the USA

www.itsapparent.org

Dedication

Proverbs 31 is a wonderful tribute to a woman whom God honors. I would like to offer the same tribute, as a dedication, to Suzie Lehman.

As verse 11 shares, "The heart of her husband trusts in her ..." and what a blessing that is to have been able to rest in the relationship in this regard.

Verse 12 shares, "She does him good, and not harm, all the days of her life," and she has been a wonderful help in all endeavors of my married life.

Verse 26 shares, "She opens her mouth with wisdom, and the teaching of kindness is on her tongue," and she has helped me, and our children, be guided to do what would most please God.

Verse 28 shares, "Her children rise up and call her blessed; her husband also, and he praises her," and what a privilege to have her live in such a way to receive these sincere accolades.

Verse 30 shares, "charm is deceitful, and beauty is vain, but a woman who fears the LORD is to be praised," and although she is charming and beautiful, her desire to put God first is captured in this verse.

As of the writing this book, It's been my privilege to have been married to my wife, Suzie, for thirty-three-and-a-half years. During that time, I can share she has been nothing short of the Proverbs 31 woman and wife to me! I therefore, in honor, dedicate this book to her!

About the Author

A counselor licensed by Association of Certified Biblical Counselors, John Lehman was born in Indiana, but spent fifteen of his first eighteen years of life in Taiwan. As an MK (missionary kid), part of his upbringing was spent in dormitory settings away from his parents. Though minimal time was spent with them during his upbringing, he was reminded about the importance of a godly marriage and home life. His parents were those who loved God and loved others. They were ones who wanted to bring out the best in each other and their children. A wonderful by-product of his parents' Christ-honoring marriage is that he was able to glean truths from their lives, as well as see them impact many others with the gospel, even if not spoken.

Early in his life, John felt called of God to *help* people, so that's what he's been doing throughout his ministry years. Initially, he thought this would be in the field of formal education, and, in essence, helping people with their marriage is an education in itself. He trusts this book will be that *help* to couples, whether engaged, newlyweds, seasoned marriage partners, or those who are having conflicts in any of those circumstances.

As God's Word reminds us in Philippians 4:13, "I can do all things through him [Christ] who strengthens me," so, with God's help, marriages can be all they should be because of all that Christ can do in enabling sinful souls to live according to the model of Christ and the church.

Acknowledgements

I would like to personally thank Dr. Tim Jordan, Pastor, Calvary Baptist Church, Lansdale, PA, and Dr. Larry Thornton, retired professor, Calvary Baptist Theological Seminary, Lansdale, PA, for their faithful instruction and encouragement throughout my early years in ministry. Much of what I have become, and have included in this book, are gleanings of truth from their pulpit and lectern.

One of the most influential books I've read, and therefore have encouraged others to implement truths found within its pages, is His Needs, Her Needs, by Willard Harley. I trust this book can be used in others' lives like it was in mine.

Craig Seelig helped in proofreading this book, helping with punctuation and sentence flow. His encouragement and direction in staying on task was a great blessing.

I thank Caroline McCausland for her attention to detail in taking this manuscript from writer and editor to being published!

I have appreciated Jim Holmes, editor and publisher consultant, who has been a confidant and resource during the questions that I have had in completing this book.

His professionalism helped get the book printed, while his personal touch helped me stay on task to get to the final product!

I thank my wife, Suzie, for encouraging me to complete this task, as she has known my passion for helping couples in their marriages, and this has allowed me to have a resource to use both pastorally and personally!

Ultimately, I thank the Lord, for He has allowed me to stay focused on this task, and has helped me to pen what I trust will be a resource to point couples to Christ, and therefore to show the world how Christ not only expects His Son and His Church to relate one to another, but also how husbands and wives are to mirror that image within their marriages.

The purpose of this book is to provide a resource so that marriages will be all that they should be for God's glory.

"He," "she," or "we"? Because the text is written with both men and women in mind, it seemed tedious to pedantically keep saying he or she, his or her, etc. So I have sometimes used the feminine gender, and other times the masculine gender, as well, at times, as using "we" and "us."

Chapter Contents

Foreword

It has been my privilege to know John Lehman for almost twenty-five years. I have known him as friend, mentor, fellow-laborer, and as the man who performed my wedding ceremony. After all those years, I can still remember his words of encouragement and advice as we went through the process of preparing for our wedding. Little did I realize that the kind truth he was sharing with us was more than merely advice for our wedding, but advice for our marriage. For twenty-one years, now, I have been performing wedding ceremonies, and countless times over those years I have repeated the advice that John shared with me. So, it is with great joy that I now recommend this book to you.

For those who are preparing for the journey of marriage, this little book contains the sound application of Scripture in practical ways that will help you navigate the joy-filled twists and turns of the most important relationship that you will ever share. For those who have traveled a while and find that your walk has become more of a march or turned into a trudge, these loving words will lighten your step by lifting your heart to remember God's purpose for your marriage. For those who perform wedding ceremonies and feel the weight of preparing young people for their most important relationship—desiring for them to experience all the joys that God intends for marriage to bring and to avoid all the disasters that selfishness and sin can usher into a home—this little book contains the vital truths that you hope to give these couples but either don't have the time in your counseling sessions, or struggle to find just the right words with which to share it.

Alan Benson, Senior Pastor, Bethel Baptist Church, Schaumburg, IL

PREFACE

Five Major Areas to Always Consider for Marriage and Intimacy

In any marriage, it is extremely important to recognize that there are certain areas which must be guided and guarded. The five areas which can attract significant challenges and difficulties are as follow: *role relationships, communication, physical relationship, finances,* and *parenting*.

You should consider these areas in some detail in order to enhance each one. You also need to recognize that if one area is failing, it will eventually erode the others. A simple illustration is found in the case of an automobile. Perhaps the car has four cylinders. It is amazing how, when one spark plug misfires, it affects the entire car. A driver doesn't discard the car because of the one fouled plug; instead an arrangement is made to repair the small misfiring part so that the entire car works properly again.

At times a marriage can use a "tune-up." There may be times when each spouse is "misfiring." Too often, couples consider difficulties as a reason to separate. Yet difficulties can actually enhance and improve the relationship when marriage partners work toward being and doing all they can for God's glory and each other's good. Resolving conflicts is a wonderful way to experience and to extend God's grace!

The purpose of this book is to provide a resource so that marriages will be all that they should be for God's glory. Love, according to Ephesians 5, is a decision of the will to give. Love specifically knows what to give to the object of affection and is not about emotionally performing it. If love turns sour, it can be made sweet again; if love's fire burns low, it can be rekindled. Love is based upon a choice, not a feeling.

The title *I Do or I Don't* brings to light exactly why marriages will or will not succeed. It is based on how willing the couple may be to follow and fulfill the marriage vows they made on their wedding day. Too often, people emphasize the wedding day rather than the marriage itself. Simply saying, "I do," and making all of these wonderful promises, does not guarantee that you will follow through. What assures the fact that you will follow through is when you commit to biblical guidelines such as these presented here.

CHAPTER 1

Marriage—under the Master

Let marriage be held in honor among all, and let the marriage bed be undefiled, for God will judge the sexually immoral and adulterous.

Hebrews 13:4

Why get married? Too many folks simply say, "Why not?" and proceed into a relationship that, as their marriage vows express, shouldn't be entered into lightly. A marriage should be entered into soberly, deliberately and with the peace of God.

Marriages today are under attack. Satan is doing all he can to erode the sanctity of marriage. Selfishness abounds. Sex is not sacred. Vows are not important. Obeying God is not considered unless it is convenient.

Marriage is a gift from God. He saw, from the beginning of time, that "it was not good that man should be alone" (Genesis 2:24). After creating Eve for Adam's companionship and joint dominion of the earth—together they were to rule over His creation—God pronounced that it was good. Just as marriage is a gift from God, in marriage, you and your spouse should be a gift, one to the other. Since God saw fit to create the woman suitable for the man, He wants man and woman to correspond to each other. It will be so much more blessed to both parties if they will fulfill their marriages as God would desire. The questions to ask are, "How valuable are you as a gift?" and "How treasured is your gift?"

The topic of this book is important because a marriage relationship is intended to reveal how Christ and the church are to respond to each other. Jesus is to be the Head of the church, and love it and cherish it. He revealed that by His very birth and death. The church is, as a result of His leadership, supposed to submit to Him. This was the specific model that God had in mind from the beginning. If that is the model, then the husband, as the head of the wife, is supposed to love and cherish her. The wife, as the church, is to submit to her earthly head and leader.

This is very difficult to comprehend, especially since we are sinners by birth and sinners by choice. Humanly speaking, it makes no sense to love like Christ and submit as to Him. However, if man is willing to base his foundation on God's Word, then he will—in a determined way—follow God's lead. By knowing what is right and being willing to do what is right, it is amazing how right the relationship will be.

LIVING IN LIGHT OF BIBLICAL PRINCIPLES

We need to be sure to note what Scripture says in determining what God wants in our own personal lives.

There are not many specific Scripture references given that specify exact ways that husbands and wives are to act and react. Just like anything else, *fundamental principles* are laced throughout Scripture. Scripture reveals how to specifically invest and live lives that would please God. It is easily understood, then, that if man is pleasing to God, as a result, he is sure to be pleasing to others.

Often people go to the passages such as Ephesians 5 to recommend what would be great qualities for husbands and wives to embrace. It is so true that husbands need to love their wives as Christ loved the church, and wives should submit to their husbands as to the Lord. However, it is extremely important to note that Scripture will do wonders in helping a person to be a godly man or woman. By the very nature of being a godly man or woman, that person will definitely be a God-honoring husband or wife. Notice, in these passages, the scriptural directive always points to God or Christ as the basis for leading and following. The men are told to love as Christ loved; the wives are told to submit as unto the Lord.

If two people base their relationship upon their human ability, they will fail. However, if instead they base their relationship upon God's will and way, they are well positioned to be the properly and biblically functioning husband and wife, enjoying success in their respective roles.

* * *

Agape love finds its reason in the one loving, not the one being loved. In other words, when one marriage partner knows that the other partner needs love, he or she will intentionally show love to that partner, no matter what. To help ensure that they stay on track in this area, agape love—that is qualitatively the same kind of love that God has for His children—finds its reason in God, not in human beings. Jesus showed the perfect example of this when He came to die for our sins. Because of His example, it is quite easy to note that we must parallel that to the best of our ability. We are to pursue, in our humanity, the agape love that God extended to us.

God gave because we needed it; He did not give because we deserved it. 1 Corinthians 13 makes the point that agape love is the only love that will endure. It is God's love, showered upon us continually and repeatedly, that causes us to want to do what is right. It is our willingness to follow His example that causes us to not only want to do it right, but also keeps us doing right!

The goal within your marital union is to please the Lord and to please your marriage partner. To do so will involve diligent effort on both accounts. As God's Word says, "A desire accomplished is sweet to the soul" (Psalm 13:19). Therefore, set out to make your desire the joy of your spouse. In practical terms, each marriage partner should always consider the following:

1) Determine to consider your marriage partner and your position (whether as husband or wife) as the highest priority. Do not let anything else get in the way. As great as children, parents and friends are, they are never to take the place away from your spouse in becoming the greatest priority;

2) Make sure that your priorities and activities are such that you still have the time necessary to know your partner as you should;

3) Think back to your dating and courting times, and how much effort you applied, showing your loved one how much you cared. However, this time of effort and initiative should not be all you ever did to make the other one feel loved and needed. Rather, you should allow that pursuit to continue, grow, and never stop. There are innumerable pressures and stresses every day in lives today. Too much of this, without a break for renewing marital love, will cause couples to focus on the minor frailties of their marriage partner and to fail to revel in their strengths. To assist in this regard, couples should do all they can to be alone for a time. Scheduling time to

"get away" was what you sought when you first were together—so do it again, and do it often!

If you are already married, enjoy this wonderful calling; if you are not yet married, may the thoughts and biblical principles on the pages that follow be of help and guidance to you as you determine whether you are to say, "I do" or "I don't"!

CHAPTER 2

Communicating in a Christlike Way

1 If then you have been raised with Christ, seek the things that are above, where Christ is, seated at the right hand of God. 2 Set your minds on things that are above, not on things that are on earth. 3 For you have died, and your life is hidden with Christ in God. 4 When Christ who is your life appears, then you also will appear with him in glory.

5 Put to death therefore what is earthly in you: sexual immorality, impurity, passion, evil desire, and covetousness, which is idolatry. 6 On account of these the wrath of God is coming. 7 In these you too once walked, when you were living in them. 8 But now you must put them all away: anger, wrath, malice, slander, and obscene talk from your mouth. 9 Do not lie to one another, seeing that you have put off the old self with its practices 10 and have put on the new self, which is being renewed in knowledge after the image of its creator. 11 Here there is not Greek and Jew, circumcised and uncircumcised, barbarian, Scythian, slave, free; but Christ is all, and in all.

12 Put on then, as God's chosen ones, holy and beloved, compassionate hearts, kindness, humility, meekness, and patience, 13 bearing with one another and, if one has a complaint against another, forgiving each other; as the Lord has forgiven you, so you also must forgive. 14 And above all these put on love, which binds everything together in perfect harmony. 15 And let the peace of Christ rule in your hearts, to which indeed you were called in one body. And be thankful. 16 Let the word of Christ dwell in you richly, teaching and admonishing one another in all wisdom, singing psalms and hymns and spiritual songs, with thankfulness in your hearts to God. 17 And whatever you do, in word or deed, do everything in the name of the Lord Jesus, giving thanks to God the Father through him.

18 Wives, submit to your husbands, as is fitting in the Lord. 19 Husbands, love your wives, and do not be harsh with them. 20 Children, obey your parents in everything, for this pleases the Lord. 21 Fathers, do not provoke your children, lest they become discouraged. 22 Bondservants, obey in everything those who are your earthly masters, not by way of eye-service, as people-pleasers, but with sincerity of heart, fearing the Lord. 23 Whatever you do, work heartily, as for the Lord and not for men, 24 knowing that from the Lord you will receive the inheritance as your reward. You are serving the Lord Christ. 25 For the wrongdoer will be paid back for the wrong he has done, and there is no partiality.

Colossians 3

Consider God's Word—Colossians 3 quoted above— an extremely helpful scriptural passage directing spouses to be the right type of person before God. As a result of being the right type of person, you will be the right type of spouse.

The first verse speaks to the importance of seeking those things which are above, which is stating and directing people to want to do what will most please God. This thought is followed by verse two which tells all to set their minds on things that are above and not on things that are on the earth. When people think and act like God desires them to, it does wonders to their human actions and reactions. Spouses need to be sure to parallel their responses with those with which Christ would be most pleased.

The third verse continues with the fact that because believers have died to their sinful desires, their lives are then hidden with Christ. So as a result of being hidden with Christ, they will be certain to have their lives reveal Christ rather than reveal self. Therefore verse 5 continues, emphasizing the importance of putting to death that which is earthly. The awful sins of our time are unambiguously addressed, and it is made abundantly clear that no one should be involved at all with sexual immorality, impurity, passion, evil desire, and covetousness, which is tantamount to idolatry.

God said from the beginning when He wrote the Ten Commandments that we were not to have any other idols before Him. Desiring anything that would go against a Holy God would mean placing human desires above God's desires. People know that they are not to be anything other than wholesome when it comes to leading a life that pleases God. God would have us therefore not desire any sexual pleasures that fall outside of marriage. He desires us to have interests and goals that promote the kingdom of God rather than promote self and self-gratification. When people want what does not please God, their lives go against a *Holy* God.

The Apostle Paul reminds his readers (see verses seven and eight) that before they trusted God, they lived unholy lives, and now those evil desires and actions must come to an end. Putting away anger, wrath, malice, slander, and obscene talk from your mouth demonstrates a godly lifestyle—when you do these things, you become a person who is easy to live with and hard to dislike. When someone does these things—putting off old sinful habits and putting on new ones—imagine what a great impact it can have on a home! Speaking negatively toward others and about others will stop altogether when a family member sincerely believes and obeys God's Word. In his list of directions, Paul includes telling his readers not to lie to one another (which can include exaggeration or harming others by speaking words that make others think less of them) and makes it clear that, in all things, people are to speak in such a manner as not to get their own way, but rather present God's way—in a marriage context, giving their spouse the benefit of the doubt.

TAKING OFF OLD GARMENTS, PUTTING ON NEW GARMENTS

In the process of putting off the bad, people must also put on the good to replace it. People don't exercise in the gym or do yard work, and then come back inside the house and stay in those clothes for the remainder of the day. They put off that which is "old" (dirty) so that they can put on that which would be "new" (clean and fresh). So God's directive to us is to put off the old, which involves anger and negative living, and to put on that which will most please Him—qualities such as gentleness and positive living. Moreover, people are to make sure that they live with compassionate hearts, kindness, humility, meekness, and patience, bearing with one another. If someone has a complaint, he should be willing to forgive, modeling and therefore illustrating the way in which the Lord saves and forgives His people. Paul goes on to say that love binds everything together in perfect harmony, a reminder that is critical, calling mankind to love, rather than be selfish.

"Let the peace of Christ rule in your hearts," is the next imperative. God wants spouses to seek peace rather than to seek their own way. He continues, urging his readers to be thankful. Spending time thanking God for what He has done will keep one from being critical. One way to help in this process is to let the Word of Christ dwell in you richly, which results in singing spiritual songs with thanksgiving to God. Being able to thank God through song will keep you from despising the negative and weaker qualities in your spouse. Finally, whatever you do should be done in the name of the Lord Jesus, giving thanks to God the Heavenly Father. After any altercation or interaction, you need to be sure whatever the outcome, it is done is in the name of Jesus, which means it will bring honor and glory to Him.

So if someone is putting off that which is "old" and is putting on that which is "new," a culture in the relationship develops which enables wives and husbands to put into practice the imperatives of verse 18: wives will be able to submit to their husbands as is fitting to the Lord, and husbands will then be able to love their wives, and not be harsh with them. Then, in completion of the whole spectrum, children will be able to obey their parents, fathers will care about their children, and even slaves will obey in everything their earthly masters require. All this is summed up in verse 23 where God says that whatever you do, you are to work heartily as for the Lord and not for men, knowing that you shall receive an inheritance from the Lord as your reward. You are serving the Lord Christ, so it only stands to reason that you will do what is right and wholesome.

"LET ME TRY TO SEE IT THE WAY YOU SEE IT."

We live before a holy God. When we realize this, and when we welcome this truth, it becomes so much easier to live in response to Him, knowing His eye is upon us so closely.

Consider a couple who desire to cultivate compassionate hearts. They want to understand everything from the other person's perspective—for this is the essence of compassion. They intentionally don't want to be selfish or in any way to put self first. This is an important step in beginning to esteem your spouse as better than yourself. Indeed, the goal of every spouse should be the kindness spoken of in this passage.

Growing closely with kindness is the quality of humility. Humble people place everything and everyone above their desires and personalities. Closely associated with this, too, is meekness, a quality that gets into action by enabling people to master their strengths and abilities, being sure that they exercise consistent self control. This is a significant way of helping the process of not putting self first. Here, patience can come to the forefront. When people patiently wait for what God and others would have in any circumstance, they are better kept from becoming bitter or anxious.

So, what about when a complaint or problem arises? The Colossians passage directs people to forgive, not grudgingly, but in the same way that Christ forgives. God says in His Word that we are to forgive as He forgives us. That is to be our pattern. To keep ourselves compassionate, humble, meek, and kind requires putting on the love and the peace of Christ. This should rule our hearts. Then as we live according to God's Word, as verse 17 reiterates, whatever we do, being humble, patient, kind, forgiving, and loving, we are to do it in the name of Jesus. We are not just to do it, but we are to do it *thankfully*. Thanking God for what He has done for us will motivate us to want to live for Him.

As husbands and wives live according to this standard, they will find it to be much easier to love and submit as is fitting to the Lord. Wives will want to submit because they desire to love God, enough to obey in that way. Husbands will love their wives and will not be harsh with them because they desire to love God and to keep His commands.

Too often, spouses forget these principles and fail to live according to the fact that God knows all and will reward all. He wants to give according to our obedience and His everlasting love. Because of His love, He wants this. However, because of His justice, He can only honor those who are ultimately honoring Him. God is not mocked—which means that people will reap what they have sown. There may be a timeframe when a man or a woman is doing wrong in a marriage and seems to be getting away with it. However, acting in principled obedience to a holy God will result in a relationship with the marriage partner that is entirely in order.

By what standard should we measure ourselves in these matters? It is so easy to compare ourselves amongst ourselves. Comparing ourselves with others tends to make us think we are a little better because we are, perhaps, obeying a little more. However, if we compare ourselves with God—and with His righteous standards—we will know that even with our very best efforts, we will never love enough to the point of really being holy. That's why God says we are to be holy like He is. This directs us to desire to be what He wants, and to pursue what He is.

CHAPTER 3

Fostering Friendship in Your Marriage

4 My beloved put his hand to the latch,
  and my heart was thrilled within me.
5 I arose to open to my beloved,
  and my hands dripped with myrrh,
my fingers with liquid myrrh,
  on the handles of the bolt.
6 I opened to my beloved,
  but my beloved had turned and gone.

The Song of Solomon 5:4–6

Song of Solomon 5:16 relates, "This is my beloved, and this is my friend." A key ingredient in any relationship is that of friendship. It is amazing how similar in character a marriage relationship can be—and indeed, should be—to be to that of early childhood best friends. There are significant parallels between the two. When a child is growing up, it is not uncommon to overlook all the faults in a best friend because of all the great qualities that friend brings into the relationship. Whether it is from failing to choose you on his kickball team or forgetting the special snack that she promised, the friendship never alters. This may be a simple illustration, but by intentionally implementing it in your marriage relationship, it may well have the effect of bringing renewed love.

If mature romance is the heart of marriage, friendship is the heart of romance. If you are not friends with your spouse, then it will be very difficult to be romantic and enjoy the precious marriage God intends you to have. Romance is not specifically a biblical term, but the joy of noting the relationship in The Song of Solomon shows that there is more to a relationship than just the physical aspect alone.

FRIENDSHIP FACTS AND FALLACIES

There are some fallacies when it comes to considering friendship in marriage. For instance, all too often, *one may think that marriage will make the friendship easier to preserve.* Yet it can be seen that by putting one's personality and talents into the pressure of living with someone else, that will definitely test that friendship to the limit. Too often it is that testing of the friendship that causes it to crumble, instead of forging it into a solid union. How is it possible to avoid the fallacy? The answer lies in eagerly and intentionally overlooking your spouse's faults, and eagerly and intentionally appreciating your spouse's strengths.

A second fallacy is that in *marriage, the spouses can cultivate their friendship without any effort*. That is going to be difficult, as the scrutiny and pressure of living with another person creates the potential for conflict. When you compare yourself to God's standard, you will see that it will require agape love to make that friendship be all that it should be. God loved us, as it is recorded in John 3:16, and as a result of that love, He gave. Therefore, as you consider a fallacy such as this—that love can be cultivated in an effortless way—it reveals that a marriage relationship will require the intentional and direct processing of extending love and grace!

As we look at the fallacies of friendship, it is extremely important, then, to consider the true facts of friendship and how these should be based on scriptural principles. Just as in the construction of a house, where a firm foundation is essential, the building of a marriage also requires a firm foundation. That foundation cannot be based on feelings and emotions, but has to be based specifically on God's Word—a foundation that will not change. The Word of God tells us that we are to pursue being holy, just like God is!

The first fact of friendship is that a *married couple is one flesh*. God says that a man must leave his father and mother and cleave to his wife and for them to become one flesh. This specifies that once this marriage union has formed, there is no separating of this relationship without harming and hurting the other party. Using the example of Superglue, you can bond two surfaces together but if it must be torn apart, it will not leave a clean break. That tearing will mean that one part of one side of the adhesion will stay with the other part, and as a result will cause great damage. God knew from the beginning that it would require a man and a woman to commit to that relationship—otherwise there is no way it would persevere. In a wedding ceremony, the marriage vows repeated should reveal the fact that the couple desires to remain married until the parting of death. The vows made to God are never to be broken. (God's Word gives some important perspectives on keeping vows in Numbers 30.)

The second fact in friendship that a marriage should have is that *the husband and wife should be of one heart.* In Ephesians 5:22 it is recorded that wives are to submit themselves to their own husbands but in a way that directly correlates with the way in which they submit to the Lord. Husbands are to love their wives as Christ loved the church and gave Himself up for her. These two verses reveal how important it is to initially establish that firm foundation. It has to be done early in the relationship. It would undoubtedly be quite easy for a wife to submit if the husband were a wonderful and compassionate leader in the home. Likewise it would be easy for the husband to love because of how wonderful his wife was being to him. If all of life remained that "bed of roses" it would be simple to continually love and submit. Since we know that life is not that easy, and that sin will get in the way of both spouses loving and submitting in response to proper and godly behavior, it is important that the husband and wife base their relationship on how Christ has given His commands and expects those commands to be followed. A Christian couple will need to base these facts—a wife's submission and a husband's love—on what God expects, and not what man feels.

Jesus gave us a wonderful opportunity to see His love extended to us when He came to earth to die for our sins. That commitment to us began even before He saw the need that was in our lives due to the sin that was so evident. When Jesus first came to earth with the intent of being born to die for us, you might think that the population would see this as a great commitment to them and would therefore respond with expressions of love and kindness. Unfortunately, the world did not see that at all! The wonder is that He loved because we needed His love—and certainly not because we deserved it. If

He had extended His love because we deserved it, we of course would never have received it!

The fact that God continues revealing in His Word that a husband and wife must also be of one mind is vitally important in showing that it becomes a joint effort in doing what is right. In Amos 3:3 God made it abundantly clear that two can walk together only if they are agreed. Using an illustration of a three-legged race highlights this quite easily. If one partner in that joint union of the three-legged race wants to go right and the other partner of that union wants to go left, they will definitely fall. Success requires working together to advance appropriately and effectively. As is true in our world, all truth is God's truth, and we see in this specific account how important it is that man must *heed* God's commands to *fulfill* God's commands!

We see, then, that the fact of friendship in marriage must be based solely and completely on the Word of God. When we choose to follow God's Word, we have chosen to accept and appreciate God's direction and blessing. Just like in our elementary school years, when we chose our best friend and then did everything in our power to promote that friendship, it will be necessary to intentionally and passionately pursue this friendship. Working from the foundation of Scripture will not make it any easier but will make it much more realistically attained because we realize we are pursuing what God desires rather than what man desires.

It is now extremely helpful to note what that formula will look like. When you put into practice what is being addressed, that is when difficulties may begin, but this also means that successful relational living is taking place.

COMMUNICATING WITH CLARITY

The first important fact is that *spouses should speak to each other face to face*. When one's feelings are of hurt or anger, and when resentment has crept in, it is very easy not to look into each other's eyes. Taking the time and the effort to consistently talk *into* a person, rather than just *to* a person, makes a lot of difference. It helps tremendously to say the person's name and look into her face. Not only is the other person's expression being noted but the one speaking will also have the opportunity of having his facial expression and body language revealed.

In Proverbs 25:11 we read that "a word fitly spoken is like apples of gold in a setting of silver." This scriptural platform came about because Solomon had a very special gift given to him. As that gift was given, he likened it to how important it is that words be given as gifts.

There have undoubtedly been times that couples can recall gifts they received when they were small children.

Those gifts may not have been the right color or style or size. When that occurred they definitely don't want to display that gift. However, when that gift had all of the appropriate ingredients, it was much easier to enjoy it. This is the same with our words. It is so important that they be spoken at the right time, in the right manner, and with the right expression. This is also true as the gifts of words are what the spouse will "wear" with them for the rest of the day. Consider this when speaking face-to-face, making sure that the words extended are truly desired and welcomed gifts.

It is therefore going to be important to notice that the principle of Scripture can be applied in this specific way. In Ephesians 5:1, God tells us to be imitators of Him as beloved children. As a result of imitating God, we will walk in that love as Christ loved us and gave Himself up for us. Giving up and extending oneself allows one to see the pattern of face-to-face enjoyment, exhortation and encouragement.

A second way to enhance this friendship in marriage is for *spouses to communicate honestly*. Usually, a person does not set out to tell a lie. Someone who desires to serve and please God does not normally want to leave the truth out of the conversation. However, when a person begins to encounter somebody else's reaction, it can be easy to alter what is said because of the reaction that will potentially occur. Because of that, there will be times that couples and spouses will avoid the topic at hand because they do not want the reaction that will occur. This is when it is so important to remember to speak the truth in love.

Usually, people are willing to speak the truth. However, when spouses get angry, it is quite easy to allow the communication to become critical and unfair. God gives the great umbrella and formula for how we speak by simply making it clear that we are to speak the truth in love. This basically reveals the fact of "truthing" in love, or guarding everything that is said under the important aspect of love. The illustration of Matthew 18 is given as an example of one person who confronts another—but with the goal of restoration. Too often, people engage in confrontation because they want to make the other person feel bad or because they want to usurp the other person and get their own way. That is not what God desires at all! He wants people to speak so that their relationships will be restored. This shows how important it is to esteem others better than self. If you are honest with yourself, it will be much easier to be honest with another person. It can be easy to convince yourself that something is wrong and therefore believe a lie about your spouse. God wants people to be honest, in word and deed!

A third aspect of friendship growing in a marriage is that *friends cultivate and enhance objectivity*. This objectivity reveals how important it is to put yourself in the other person's position. When you can see what is transpiring in the other person's life, you become much less selfish and become much more loving. As God has said in His Word, He loved us and therefore gave to us. This kind of objectivity helps you to want to help the other person become all he or she can be for God's glory. When you make that as a goal, then all your efforts are based on encouragement and edification rather than trying to selfishly get your own way. When you see your spouse as God sees, you will more likely extend unconditional love. You will consistently want the best for your spouse. There will not be any jealousy or desire to selfishly promote your own goals. Your desire will then be to help the other person continually and effectively become more and more conformed to Christ's image.

One friend will almost certainly desire to help another friend to improve. Promoting growth in another individual means taking your eyes off of yourself and seeking to help the other one be better. The principle is simply that of esteeming others better than yourself (see Philippians 2:3). Such a verse comes to mind when I consider helping someone to become better because of the influence I may have in that person's life. It is quite easy to get caught up in selfish desires and personal interests. At all times it is important to realize that your partner for life needs to be helped in all areas.

It is extremely important that *marriage partners make sure that they are sharing their inmost thoughts*. One marriage partner should never share something of a personal nature with someone else if he or she has not already shared it with the other. Inappropriately sharing these inmost thoughts may lead to an emotional attachment, and too often emotional attachments may lead to physical affection as well. Keep to the rule that you will never share with a person of the opposite gender something that you have not already shared with your own spouse. At the same time, be very mindful that you are willing to be vulnerable and so share these different concerns and fears in order to continue to build a very close relationship.

One friend will *set aside personal comforts so that the other friend will have such*. That is extremely important as it again reveals how important it is to desire to put the other person above your own desires. This is when you begin considering such little things as who gets up first and who begins certain daily rituals so the other one can sleep just a little longer. Or perhaps it is choosing to enjoy or prepare meals that may not have been your priority or personal choice but for the good of your spousal friendship you set aside your own personal interests and comforts for the other's benefit.

It is also extremely important that *spouses give each other their full support.* That may reveal itself in not being competitive with who has spare time or free time, or who receives certain commendations, accolades or advancements. As God has said in His Word, we are to rejoice with those who rejoice (see Romans 12:15). It is at such times that spouses should specifically show their friendship in rejoicing over the recognition of their marriage partner. Giving full support to the other will likewise reveal itself when it comes to taking vacations or having families to visit. Keeping records of who went where and when will only cause difficulties. God has said that we are not to compare ourselves among ourselves for if we do we may be called fools (see 2 Corinthians 10:12). When one spouse does not give undivided and complete support to the other, difficulties are ready to introduce themselves.

Not only will friends desire to put aside their own comforts and be willing to give their full support to their spouse, but *they will also desire to meet the other person's needs.* Consider your elementary school friends and reflect on that wonderful relationship. After you do this, you will realize that your childhood friends did not elevate themselves and desire their own way but instead were often desiring the best for their friend. God's Word does say that we can do all things through Christ who strengthens us—see Philippians 4:13. That reveals that we can get by with certain of our desires not being met. God says, through Paul that "... having food and raiment let us be therewith content" (1 Timothy 6:8, KJV). But if we sincerely desire to meet our spouse's needs, we will actually find great joy in the meeting of those needs. This will be a great fulfillment to the partner who is extending himself or herself. As God has said, we *do* reap what we sow (see Galatians 6:7). As one willingly gives, it will be very easy for the other to reciprocate that as well.

Friends desire to help their spouse reach full potential. Often couples will get married prior to certain degree completions or vocational attainment. There may be a time when both spouses are working diligently so that they can advance to the next level of education or vocation. This is the time that one spouse will need to recognize how important it is to help the other spouse in that pursuit. As one helps the other in a pursuit, it turns out to be a blessing in one's own life.

Friends are also completely loyal and committed to their friends. This means that they will not think ill of their spouse in any circumstance. They are going to believe only that which is wholesome and good about their spouse. They are only going to encourage and uplift their spouse; they are not going to think anything ill at all.

As spousal friends, it is extremely important for you to *have a complete attitude of accepting your spouse exactly "as is,"* with no aspirations of what that person can become because of your personal influence. Spouses have chosen each other based on their personal and previous relationship. All of the strengths and qualities which originally attracted them to each other need to continually be enhanced and supported. As marriages begin, spouses are looking through rose-colored lenses and seeing only the good in their spouse. Unfortunately, after a time of marriage, if they are not careful, they might begin to look through microscopic lenses and highlight and accentuate the negative factors. Accept one another for the reason you got married. Enjoy that gift and continue to appreciate all that you are to the other.

Friends are completely open about everything. There should never be a time when a question is asked and a complete and wholesome answer is not given. Be open about strengths as well as weaknesses. It is much easier to talk about each other's strengths because those are the areas that initially attracted you to each other. Weaknesses, although at times not spoken about, are undoubtedly known by the other person as well. Be willing to share failures and sorrow as well as goals and desires to accomplish. Even if these desires are not accomplished, try again. As Proverbs 13:12 says, "Hope deferred makes the heart sick, but a desire fulfilled is a tree of life." When the desire is accomplished, it it is definitely "sweet to the soul" (Proverbs 13:19).

Finally, *friends need to be continually enjoyable*! That enjoyment is undoubtedly what initially attracted you to each other. You had fun and laughed at each other and with each other at important and unimportant situations. So, seek to make the other person's life enjoyable and desire above all else to be that friend that "sticks closer than a brother" as it is recorded in Proverbs 17:17, KJV. As friends seek to make friends, they are always putting their best foot forward. That should not stop once the wedding day is over. In fact, that extension of oneself should be desired even more than ever!

An illustration for all of these is to consider two friends stranded together in a rubber raft in the middle of the ocean. In that raft there is only one bottle of water. As the day wears on, the threat begins from one rower to the other that if he drinks too much water, she is going to poke a hole in his boat. Unfortunately, that rower does not realize that poking a hole in the other person's raft is really poking a hole in her own. So, when spouses become selfish and look for their specific and personal needs and desires to be met, they are crippling their joint relationship. Selfishness will never help promote a relationship. Selfishness only brings it down. In these types of relationships, each spouse needs to realize that the goal should be to help the friend and spouse to be all that he or she can be and, in working toward this, to enhance the relationship!

PREVENTING FRIENDSHIP FAILURE

Just as we have looked at the formula that we should have in our friendship, it is extremely important to look at ways that friendship can fail.

The first is that *friends can become selfish.* When you desire your own personal interests and own aspirations, you don't have time to look out for the other person's. That kind of selfishness will impact the manner spouses begin to withdraw from each other. It will also impact your spouse as she will simply begin reciprocating what you are either giving or withholding. One of the greatest ways to keep from being selfish is to look out for the other person's interests and desire, above all else, to help her to reach full potential in all realms of life, whether personal, physical, emotional, or spiritual. If you become selfish, your spouse will become selfish, but if you are willing to be unselfish, that same characteristic is sure to become evident in your marriage partner, too.

If friends are not careful, *they may become overly possessive of their belongings and time.* Many times this occurs because, throughout their life, they have had their own room, their own clothes and their own money. There is nothing wrong with having had those, unless they forget that the only reason they ever had anything was because God had entrusted them to a family that was able to provide them.

To put this more specifically to you, because of God's ongoing blessing, He has given you the means and the resources to still have these things. By realizing that the only thing you really possess is the privileged opportunity of a personal relationship with Jesus Christ, that should motivate you to continually give, just as He gave to us. John 3:16 reminds us that God loved the world so much that He gave His only begotten Son!

Friends must be very careful not to become jealous of each other. No one ever set out to be a failure. However, along the way people can become so jealous that they want to be the only ones to be lauded and appreciated. Therefore, when they see their spouse receive accolades, they become jealous over the fact that they themselves are not receiving the same recognition and praise. This is the time to remember that as a married couple you are one flesh—so commendation of one is really commendation of both! Jealousy will keep you from encouraging and motivating your loved one, so be sure you get rid of that awful characteristic.

Friends should be very careful that they do not become angry and sin. God has said in His Word that when we are angry, we are not to sin (Ephesians 4:26). God has revealed that, because He is a God of justice, He is the One to exercise righteous indignation. God's wrath is never meted out inappropriately. The only reason our wrath is meted out inappropriately is because we are fallen and will sin if we speak and react in the way we feel we would like to. God, of course, lets us realize that we cannot be supportive and encouraging, and destructive and angry all at the same time. Many of these emotions are mutually exclusive. So, be mindful when you feel or use such anger! When it arises, rather channel your energies into responding to or repairing any difficulties that may have occurred.

It is essential for friends to continually desire to keep away from bitterness. God tells us that bitterness eats like a canker, which means it keeps you from enjoying the pleasures of life. That bitterness of the soul will keep you from enjoying your own pursuits and, in turn, it will make you frustrated at the accomplishments of your spouse. It is important to realize that bitterness occurs because of many of the emotions just discussed. A person who is not selfish, possessive, jealous, or angry will not become bitter.

Friends also need to *be very mindful that they do not become envious*. There is a slight difference in all of these different forms of jealousy. A person who is envious is someone who perceives that another person has more than he or she has and, as a result, wants to get one up on the other. This should never occur! One marriage partner is to desire, above all else, to encourage and support the other. There will be no way for envy and encouragement to exist at the same time. If you are sincerely pursuing the best for the other person, you will never be envious of that person's successes. Instead, you will rejoice in the things accomplished.

CHAPTER 4

The Loveliness of Love

1 If I speak in the tongues of men and of angels, but have not love, I am a noisy gong or a clanging cymbal. 2 And if I have prophetic powers, and understand all mysteries and all knowledge, and if I have all faith, so as to remove mountains, but have not love, I am nothing. 3 If I give away all I have, and if I deliver up my body to be burned, but have not love, I gain nothing.

4 Love is patient and kind; love does not envy or boast; it is not arrogant 5 or rude. It does not insist on its own way; it is not irritable or resentful; 6 it does not rejoice at wrongdoing, but rejoices with the truth. 7 Love bears all things, believes all things, hopes all things, endures all things.

8 Love never ends. As for prophecies, they will pass away; as for tongues, they will cease; as for knowledge, it will pass away. 9 For we know in part and we prophesy in part, 10 but when the perfect comes, the partial will pass away. 11 When I was a child, I spoke like a child, I thought like a child, I reasoned like a child. When I became a man, I gave up childish ways. 12 For now we see in a mirror dimly, but then face to face. Now I know in part; then I shall know fully, even as I have been fully known.

13 So now faith, hope, and love abide, these three; but the greatest of these is love.

1 Corinthians 13

A great principle for all couples in their understanding and pursuing of a quality, godly relationship in their marriage is to base their marriage on 1 Corinthians 13. As is noted in this chapter, no matter what you may have in the way of strengths or skills, if you do not have love, it is basically worthless. This reveals how important love really is. Marriages may have a lot of resources, a great appearance, and vocational success, but if there is not love and friendship in that relationship, it will be very shallow. To keep enhancing that relationship, take a moment to be sure that your love is based on 1 Corinthians 13.

The first strength that love reveals is that of being *patient*. Patient people are those who are not easily riled when things do not go their way, right away. Their goal is to take their time and constantly extend and reveal love, no matter what is taking place. By being patient, they will wait and hear out the other person and evaluate the entire circumstance before becoming frustrated and allow any improper expression in reaction to occur. Love is patient!

The second strength that is expressed to the Corinthian church is that of being *kind*. A kind person will want what is best for the other person. He will be mindful that, no matter what the situation is, or what has occurred, he will want to make sure that the other person does not feel offended or hurt. He is committed to being helpful, no matter what has occurred to him. Love is kind!

The Scriptures continue by showing us that love is actually very *protective*. A person showing love desires to only believe that which is the best interpretation of the other person's character or actions. Even if something is said that might be to the contrary, he prefers to believe that the small and insignificant situation definitely has an explanation. In displaying this spirit of protecting the other, he will not jump to conclusions and consider the other person guilty before the entire circumstance has been investigated and is known. And even if the whole circumstance is known and "guilt" is assessed, it still doesn't mean that that person isn't valuable. No matter what sin has taken place, it can be covered. Love is protecting!

Spouses should always be *trusting*. In a day when lives are so busy and we have so many distractions in our lives, there may be opportunities not to trust the other person. Trusting at times will require intentionally believing— believing what is best in that other person, rather than immediately disbelieving, is the best way to relate. Love is trusting!

The Apostle Paul's next point is that love actually *hopes all things*. Hoping means that one is actually anticipating the good qualities in that other person. In essence, it believes in the potential of that person. It is important to have the other's best interest at heart so as then to be able to literally hope that everything that is taking place is going to be for the better. When you do this, you will demonstrate that you believe in the integrity of the other. Love is hoping!

1 Corinthians 13:7 ends this section making the point that love *endures all things*. Love will not give up on the other person. Love knows that the other person needs to continually be the object of one's pursuit. A person who perseveres does not give up. If you do not give up, as God's Word says, you will reap if you faint not. Consider Galatians 6:9—"And let us not grow weary of doing good, for in due season we will reap, if we do not give up." No matter what the circumstances are, difficulties will continue to demonstrate the reality of the qualities of love outlined in 1 Corinthians 13. Love perseveres.

In addition to telling us what love *is*, 1 Corinthians 13 also tells us what love *is not*. Love is *not envious*. We see in verse 4 that love is not envious. That underscores the point made that friends should not fail by being jealous or envious. This goes along with the thought of 1 Corinthians 13 in wanting the other person to succeed and to be better. When one is constantly encouraging others, there is no place for envy. Love is not envious!

Love in a marriage union is *not boastful*. It is vital for you to always realize that anything and everything you have received has only been from the hand of God! God would not have anyone to boast, except in the cross of Jesus Christ (see Galatians 6:14). If the boasting is on how loving God was and how great He is, then that is not wrong. When you boast about your own personal attainments within marriage, you are leaving out the fact that God gave you the opportunity and the ability to express those skills. Love is not boastful!

Love is *not proud*. Love is not going to consider accepting anything that is accomplished because of its own personal merit. Verse 4 is clear that love is not arrogant. Therefore, it follows that love is not going to be self-seeking or self-promoting. A person who esteems others better than himself surely wants to promote the best in the other— there is no concern about what he does or does not have. Love is not proud!

Love is *not rude*. A person who is rude certainly does not consider the interests or the needs of the other person and will cut in on conversations or usurp the other person's own point of view, often regardless of what is taking place. The main goal is to point out the fact that she is present and that she really is quite an accomplished person. How important it is to realize that if you love God and love others, you cannot be rude. Love is not rude!

Love is *not self-seeking*. If you are a person who is self-seeking, as Scripture says, you are one who insists on your own way. That reveals how important it is to always want what is best for your spouse. For marriage to continue in that covenant made before God, you must constantly remember that, together with your marriage partner, you have already pledged "for better or worse, for richer, for poorer, in sickness and in health, until death do us part." What a spur to constantly remain faithful and true. If you deviate from those vows made at the altar, this reveals that you are seeking your own way rather than what is best for your spouse. Love is not self-seeking!

Paul continues this short chapter, directing us to see that love is *not irritable* or is *not angry*. A person who is angry is one who has not gotten his or her way and therefore wants to hurt and bring the other person down. The angry person wants to appear in a better light. If you really and sincerely want what is best for your spouse, you are not going to be concerned with the times that she loses heart or has to face difficulties. Instead, you will desire to help her to be all she can be and therefore you will not get upset at those times. Love is not angered!

Finally, love does *not find fault*. Verse 6 makes it clear that love does not rejoice at wrongdoing. When couples initiate their relationship, they are trying to put the best foot forward. Each believes everything that is good and wholesome about the other person. Unfortunately, once you are married, you may begin to find fault. The worst thing about finding fault is that you begin, and then continue, identifying and tracking and enumerating those faults. If you allow that to build up, it will definitely cause a spirit of bitterness—and bitterness will certainly keep couples from loving. Do not rejoice at wrongdoing. Love does not find fault!

Verse seven concludes the list of love's wonderful characteristics—it endures difficulties, gives the best possible interpretation of events, and hopes and endures all things.

1 Corinthians 13 is a wonderful chapter for couples to consider together. It articulates the qualities of divine love; and it provides a reference grid for husbands and wives—a series of benchmarks—for them to work from in endeavoring to develop an exemplary marriage to God's glory.

CHAPTER 5

The Intricacies of Intimacy

18 Then the LORD God said, "It is not good that the man should be alone; I will make him a helper fit for him." 19 Now out of the ground the LORD God had formed every beast of the field and every bird of the heavens and brought them to the man to see what he would call them. And whatever the man called every living creature, that was its name. 20 The man gave names to all livestock and to the birds of the heavens and to every beast of the field. But for Adam there was not found a helper fit for him. 21 So the LORD God caused a deep sleep to fall upon the man, and while he slept took one of his ribs and closed up its place with flesh. 22 And the rib that the LORD God had taken from the man he made into a woman and brought her to the man. 23 Then the man said,

"This at last is bone of my bones and flesh of my flesh; she shall be called Woman, because she was taken out of Man."

24 Therefore a man shall leave his father and his mother and hold fast to his wife, and they shall become one flesh. 25 And the man and his wife were both naked and were not ashamed.

Genesis 2:18–25

CAUSES FOR LACK OF INTIMACY

One of the most important truths to recognize is that God created! As God created the world, on the different days and different ways that He created, He always concluded by saying that it was good. However, when Adam recognized that he did not have another person to correspond to, God said it was "not good" that man should be alone. God already had a plan for that. He put Adam into a deep sleep and opened up the body that He had just created. He removed a rib from his side, and used that rib to create woman. Following that creation is the verse which states that "a man shall leave his father and his mother and hold fast to his wife, and they shall become one flesh."

It is extremely important to recognize that God created men and women for intimate marriages. Today, too often the word "intimate" only refers to a relationship of a physical nature. That is definitely one part of being intimate, but even more so than in the physical realm is the more profound closeness that man has initially with his Creator. Generally speaking, if people have an intimate relationship with God, they have a close relationship which allows them to be able to access Him in His role as Creator and Maker, and request His assistance in this present life. God initially created Adam to be someone with whom He could relate and communicate. Therefore, it is extremely important to understand why it was so devastating that man severed that relationship on falling into sin when disobeying God's commandment.

Because God is a relational Being, He created man as a social being, to relate to Him, to relate to his mate, and to relate to others. The first marriage was actually a combination—or one could even say, in a sense, a triangulation—involving God, Adam and Eve. Once woman was created out of man, man responded to her with great joy, noticing simultaneously the sameness and differences. This would allow for closeness—that is, intimacy—but also for individual identity. For one to have a truly intimate marriage it must be intimate, or close, in all aspects.

As may be noticed in Genesis 2:24, the first marriage was established as a new social unit, was established on a commitment (Matthew 2:14–16; Proverbs 2:1, 2:17, Romans 7; 1 Corinthians 7), and was established for oneness and intimacy. Because sin entered the world, that closeness became severed; and because of sin, the desire to be rightly related to God and do all that He had commanded was severed as well. Man soon realized that, because of his sin, he had affected his wonderful relationship with God, and therefore he sought a way for recovery. Unfortunately, he was not able to succeed in this pursuit. Yet God, because of His love, revealed His desire to reunite in that relationship. God, even from the beginning of time, initiated a plan that man would be able to receive forgiveness and reconciliation. As a result of that, he would be able to have the penalty for his sins fully paid and be brought back to a complete and full relationship with God.

This is extremely important to realize because, as God progressively revealed in Scripture—especially to be seen in the letters to the Ephesians and Colossians—He drew a parallel between the relationship of Christ and the church, on the one hand, with that of a husband and wife, on the other. This reveals to us that there is a perfect pattern in marriage to follow. If husbands and wives simply followed that pattern, they would be able to have the intimate relationship that God designed and purposed.

Unfortunately, because of sin, people would see the failings and frailties in their spouse and highlight those weaknesses—especially so in the realm of the relationship between a husband and a wife. Rather than noticing and focusing on the wrong in each other, they should be concentrating on the great gift that God gave them in revealing a pattern for love. Just as Christ loved the church, and just as the church submits to Christ, here is a wonderful model for culturing and nurturing a relationship of intimacy.

Although lack of intimacy is wrong, it is helpful to be aware of some of the reasons for it.

First, in our world today we have culturally conditioned people. There are men and women in marriages who are conditioned by the wrong values and beliefs of our society rather than being conditioned by Scripture. It may be seen in Ephesians 5:29 that husbands are told to nourish and cherish their wives.

Secondly, in this general context, women are told in 1 Peter 3:1 that they are able to win or influence their husbands based on their lifestyle and not on their words. Too often today, men and women will respond and react according to how they have been brought up as well as how they have been influenced in their early childhood. Some homes do not extend much physical affection—they are environments where there is a lack of touching, hugging, kissing, eye contact, expressing feelings, and hearing the words "I love you." Because of some of this kind of conditioning, it is easy for the people who experienced it to come into their marriages without properly interacting with and loving their spouse. Our society, by the very nature of doing this, causes much harm. Spouses will pattern themselves from what they have observed. At the same time, spouses are not let off the hook for reacting this way. It is their specific responsibility to extend themselves in revealing love and compassion for the other.

Just as our culture has conditioned men and women not to reveal love as they ought to, it has also impacted couples to be discontent in their status of life. God has said "that whatever state that we are in we are to be content" (Philippians 4:11). Unfortunately there are so many comparisons made today that most young couples will consider how little they have and how much someone else has. If they haven't noticed it before they get married, they certainly will after they do! Whether this is by observing advertisements, friends, or society, they will perceive that they do not have as much as the other people do. Because of that, they may well become unhappy with the way their husbands live or the level of economic standing they have attained. Soon they believe they don't have all that they deserve they should have, and find that they are in conflict because of discontentment. Once people become discontented, they begin to become manipulative or competitive. They begin to love themselves and, as they begin to become aware of what they *don't* have, instead of loving God and noting that the things they *do indeed have* are as a result of God's goodness!

Another reason for lack of intimacy is that there are disillusioned couples today who have based their relationships on their own emotional feelings—romantic ones—toward each other. Although romance is—and can be a special part of the marriage relationship—it can be the downfall of the marriage. The term romance speaks of the emotional closeness caused because of sexual attraction. It is superficial and it is not guaranteed to achieve personal intimacy in marriage. While the couple may have that sexual attraction, it is not the entirety of life. Therefore, when a lack of romance becomes evident, the marriage partners may believe they need someone else in their life and so they start to look outside of the wonderful parameters that God has given them in marriage.

Couples must be careful to seek and follow the goals that they set out for themselves. There will be times that they will not only have different goals but they will pursue different levels. As Amos 3:3 notes—"How can two walk together except they be agreed?"—if they are disagreeing in their goals, then it will certainly mean that they will be in disagreement too often. When couples do not see eye to eye, and do not work at overcoming the selfishness that personal satisfaction brings, they will continue to be less and less intimate.

Sometimes couples harm the relationship because they build walls between themselves. Sometimes the reason for these walls is that men and women are fearful—based on their own feelings and pursuits—that they will not be accepted by their spouse. A wife with this fear may keep herself from revealing weaknesses, faults, inadequacies, sins, existing differences, etc., from her husband, as well as becoming demeaning because of how short she fears she may fall from her husband's expectations. Similarly, because of these kinds of shortcomings, husbands may be afraid that they will be rejected, exploited, dominated, lose their identity, or have the information used against them by their wives. These walls have to be torn down; otherwise they will become terrible prisons of loneliness. That's why an intimate relationship is so important. These difficulties are bound to arise, and if couples are as close as they ought to be, these fears may be experienced, but they will have the effect of drawing each other closer rather than keeping each other apart.

People in general are lazy. Because of this, it is easy to not want to work at making a marriage all that it can and should be. Marriage is a task that two people have to work at together, in selfless ways. To experience intimacy takes real effort. It is important to reflect back on how much energy was expended during courtship and dating and consider doing those same things now. This may well include using cards, flowers, planning dates, spending time cooking or cleaning together, or making extra efforts to appear attractive. These principles can be found in Galatians 6:7–9 and Ephesians 5:23–33. Rather than being a lazy lover, one should be an active lover, as Christ was to the church. He revealed agape love, which was because of the need of His people, not because of the worthiness of His people. It is much easier to want to be loved than to do the loving; and so it takes real effort to extend love and grace and to esteem the other person better than oneself. The dividends of doing so far outweigh the dividends of being selfish!

Too often, marriages have either listless or loud communicators within them. Without communication, no marriage will experience intimacy. There will also be no intimacy with the wrong kind of communication. Therefore it is extremely important to note that lack of intimacy can come about because of a lack of communication or because of wrong types of communication. Vulnerability that allows a person to share feelings, thoughts, deep hurts, and great joys is essential in establishing and maintaining a climate of closeness. Hostile feelings over conflicts, when suppressed, develop resentment, frustration, depression and withdrawal. Ephesians 4:15 refers to speaking the truth in love, Colossians 3:19 tells men to love their wives and not be bitter against them, and Ephesians 4:29 tells us that we are not to let corrupt communication proceed out of our mouth. Those are exact statements and indicate how important it is to be the right type of communicator—and why. When communication is not proper, it creates lack of intimacy.

Finally, there are, unfortunately, men and women who want to control the situation. They want their way and they want it on their timetable and for their own betterment. Those who insist on this level of control certainly keep intimacy from existing or flourishing. There has to be a relationship of mutuality and equality (see 1 Peter 3:7, Galatians 3:28). A person who wants to control others makes those within his influence feel inferior and brings about discouragement. A husband or wife treated as nothing will reveal the same! A leader, in biblical terms, is a servant just like Christ—see Matthew 20:26–28. This Scripture reveals to us how important it is to know that whatever is taking place, it should always bring glory to God.

PRACTICAL STEPS TO REINSTATE INTIMACY

For a couple to restore this intimacy in their marriage, they must realize it is a choice. God Himself has revealed that to us—He wanted us to know Him and to love Him.

He revealed this by showing agape love which is selfless love. He loved us because of our need, not because of our worth. For folks to become more intimate in their marriage, they must demonstrate the same kind of love. John 13:17, 34–35 are verses that show us that, even if they don't feel like this, they must do this to do right.

In taking steps toward intimacy, it is extremely important that couples apply God's Word in their life. 2 Timothy 3:16–17 makes it clear that we must be looking into God's Word, the Bible. We are to study His Word so that we may be approved and provide service. We are able to study God's Word in the area of doctrine and of instruction and then follow through with scriptural principles. When couples are willing to apply Scripture to their lives, they are willing to repent, request, and extend forgiveness.

Admitting that you are wrong is never easy. Prior to confessing, you must be willing to admit you are wrong. In the middle of any type of lifestyle, it is always going to happen that someone is wrong. If you are wrong, you will begin to understand the errors that you have brought into your life, and then you will begin to desire, above all else, to seek restoration. If a failure has occurred, it is extremely important for forgiveness to be extended and for bitterness not to be harbored. Forgiveness must be patterned after the means and ways that God has shown!

Once you have repented, and sought and received forgiveness, you have to begin the important process of restructuring your behavior pattern that destroyed the intimacy you once had. As you look into Matthew 7:2–5, Ephesians 4:22, and Colossians 3:8, you will see that it reveals how important it is for folks to use God's Word as a resource to be and do all that God would have for them. As a couple, you must apply God's Word consistently in your marriage if you are to be intimate as God desires.

To maintain a relationship that parallels that of Christ and the church, it is extremely important that each mate accepts the other exactly as he or she is. Often, what draws a couple together can become an issue when one of them recognizes that that the other wonderful individual actually has certain weaknesses. All people, because of sin, have weaknesses. All people, because they are made of flesh, have weaknesses. There is no one who is going to avoid marrying someone with weaknesses. Therefore, it is extremely important to realize how Christ accepts us, as the pattern for our accepting our spouse just as he or she is. John 6:36, Matthew 11:28, and 1 Peter 5:7 specifically make clear to us how Christ accepted us. He took us exactly as we were; He did not have any stipulations that we had to be a certain way before He would be willing to extend His forgiveness and love to us. Therefore, for a couple to continue on this path of intimacy in their marriage, they must accept their mates just as they are!

It is also extremely important that couples not only accept their mate but appreciate their mate, too. It is vital for them to praise each other for the unique qualities introduced into the marriage. Both spouses have come from different environments. They have had different upbringings. They are created fearfully and wonderfully, and yet are unique in their own right. Because of that, it is really important to recognize the strengths that each has brought into this marriage relationship. These strengths can actually be a complement to the other. As couples seek to use their strengths in their marriage to be all they can for God's glory, they will continually mature, grow, and make their relationship even stronger because of their contributions. When there is such emphasis on praise and encouragement within a marriage, there is no time or desire to be negative. (See 1 Peter 3:7, Proverbs 31:28, 30, Proverbs 14:1 Song of Solomon 5:9–16.) Appreciate your mate!

Whenever relationships increase in their affection, there always begins to be physical and emotional affection shown. It is important to reveal affection for your spouse. See 1 Peter 3:7, Ephesians 5:25, 28, 33, Titus 2:4, Romans 12:10, and Song of Solomon 1:2, 3:1, all being passages that show how much one can continue to show high esteem for one's spouse. Initially a spouse is to nourish— which means "to care for with the purpose of bettering." Couples, by the very act of getting married, surely desire that together they will be able to serve God much better than if they were to remain single. The focus of this kind of nourishing is to help the other be better than he or she would have been alone. Couples need to cherish each other, holding each other in high esteem.

Affection can also be shown by cheering your spouse onward. Deuteronomy 24:5 shows the importance of cheering another person. This has the idea of encouraging the other person so he or she can perform and accomplish more with the spouse's help than would have been possible alone. Presenting the idea of affection, Romans 12:10 talks about how we are to be kindly affectionate one to another. We are to enhance another individual because of our involvement in that person's life. If this is so in a general way, how much more important it is for there to be this type of affection shown in a marriage relationship. Show affection for your spouse in the cheering-on process!

To achieve proper marital intimacy, you will also have to agree on daily goals and life goals. To help your marriage partner become more intimate in your relationship, you should consider yourselves together as partners and companions—united as one in soul and mind. You enter a partnership with the purpose of making that body that has been joined in union in marriage even better than you would have been as two separate individuals. Such unity should be the norm in marriage. Couples need to recognize what a vital role they play in their relationship and how important it is for them to help each other improve because of their involvement on a personal level.

When God addresses this fact in Genesis 2:24—that a husband and wife are to leave their father and mother and cleave to each other and become one flesh—He is speaking about that in all aspects of marriage. It is easy to consider the one-flesh union to highlight and accentuate the physical relationship. That is a true statement, but a couple should use that closeness and should apply that to every aspect of their relationship. Agreeing on daily goals and life goals in a joint fashion will certainly assist in marital intimacy. Couples need to agree on daily and life goals!

A significant way to become intimate is to acknowledge that your mate should be your best friend. There is a parallel in The Song of Solomon 5:16. Consider the fact that as a married couple you have made a covenant before the Lord. If you vow a vow, and fail to keep it, you are worse than a fool. Everyone knows that a fool doesn't follow advice and doesn't do what is right. To enhance this is extremely important because it is a covenant before the Lord. In marriage ceremonies, the comment is often made that the couple is entering into this covenant before God and man. One of the most important aspects of a marriage ceremony is the people that are witnesses to the covenant that has been made.

Not only is this a covenant before the Lord, but it is also a one-flesh union. There is not to be anyone else in this union. God makes reference to the physical relationship and states specifically that the marriage bed is to be undefiled (Hebrews 13:4). That reveals that this one physical flesh union is provided for the couple's pleasure and to bring glory to God. That one-flesh union goes way beyond just the joining of the flesh, communicating to the soul and spirit as well. Because of this, a couple needs to share memories and blessings together, by acknowledging a variety of ways that God has worked in their lives in the past. This will assist in a great way as they reflect on God's goodness to them and count God's blessings.

Not only should they share these memories and blessings, but they really need to have a prayer life together. "The prayer of a righteous man avails much" (James 5:16), and as this couple praises and asks God to help them, it will become a wonderful habit. Even in difficult times they will seek God and make certain that their responses and reactions are pleasing to Him, which in turn will definitely please the spouse.

It is also helpful for a couple to share responsibilities within their marriage union. There is ownership in becoming a married couple and therefore it is important for both the husband and the wife to work together. This is necessary so that their union will be all that it can be for God's glory and for each other's good. God actually commands us to love our spouse. Initially he tells men to love their wives as Christ loved the church. That shows how important a decision love is. Later in Titus 2, there is a parallel principle, one in which the apostle urges that older women are to teach the younger women how to love their husbands. And if that is not enough, God actually says we are to love our neighbors as ourselves—in life, there is no neighbor that lives any closer than a spouse! If you are tempted to be selfish, rather elevate your marriage partner. That will make love flow the way it should!

Finally, God has actually made it clear that there is an "heirship" that this couple has together. Thus it is written in 1 Peter 3:7 that the husband is helping his wife as an "heir of the grace of life." The husband is to be leading his wife so that she is prepared to be presented to God. She should be better because of his influence. The wife is to submit to her husband as to the Lord, which allows her to recognize that what she is doing can bring glory to God by bringing honor to her husband.

CHAPTER 6

Loving Leadership and Submission with Satisfaction

15 Look carefully then how you walk, not as unwise but as wise, 16 making the best use of the time, because the days are evil. 17 Therefore do not be foolish, but understand what the will of the Lord is. 18 And do not get drunk with wine, for that is debauchery, but be filled with the Spirit, 19 addressing one another in psalms and hymns and spiritual songs, singing and making melody to the Lord with your heart, 20 giving thanks always and for everything to God the Father in the name of our Lord Jesus Christ, 21 submitting to one another out of reverence for Christ.

22 Wives, submit to your own husbands, as to the Lord. 23 For the husband is the head of the wife even as Christ is the head of the church, his body, and is himself its Savior. 24 Now as the church submits to Christ, so also wives should submit in everything to their husbands.

25 Husbands, love your wives, as Christ loved the church and gave himself up for her, 26 that he might sanctify her, having cleansed her by the washing of water with the word, 27 so that he might present the church to himself in splendor, without spot or wrinkle or any such thing, that she might be holy and without blemish.[a] 28 In the same way husbands should love their wives as their own bodies. He who loves his wife loves himself. 29 For no one ever hated his own flesh, but nourishes and cherishes it, just as Christ does the church, 30 because we are members of his body.

Ephesians 5:15–30

ROLE RELATIONSHIPS—OUR GIFT TO MODEL CHRIST AND THE CHURCH

The first area that we must think about is that of role relationships. Consider the importance of the relationship that God wanted to have with Adam. This shows us how important that aspect of the relationship was. God wanted to be able to relate to man, and the way for this to occur was for there to be a mutual response one to another. God has given us strict instructions in His Word, and when we follow those instructions, the relationship becomes properly established.

Words to Men

The first of the two roles to look at in the relationship is that of the husband. The husband is to have two major roles in the marriage: leadership and love.

LEADERSHIP: First, he is to provide *leadership* in the marriage. Leadership is necessary. There is no way that any organization or group of people will ever advance without a leader. A family will not know what to do without there being a leader. God has ordained man to be just that leader, and this is clear from Ephesians 5:23 as well as 1 Corinthians 11:3. The leader, of course, must make certain that he has a goal and a plan. For a Christian, that goal and plan must be centered on God's Word and must follow the principles of doing that which God wants man to do.

Leadership is certainly required, but the leader is not to be one who lords himself over the ones he leads. Leadership should be considered a *service* to the ones that are being led. We notice this in Matthew 20:20–28, John 13:1–15, as well as in Philippians 2:6–8. Christ came to this world not to be served but to serve. He often stated that the greatest would be one who is servant. In Scripture, Christ compares His relationship to the church with the relationship between a husband and wife. Therefore, if Christ came to this world to serve, then the husband, although himself a leader, must realize that service is an extremely important part of that leadership. A husband should be encouraged by recognizing the fact that his service to his family is one which God has ordained for him to perform. He shouldn't regret or detest this but rather welcome and embrace the fact that he can serve his family.

Leadership also involves the principle of *continuous association*. Stated simply, this emphasizes the fact that you must be with those you lead. Leadership may just be thought of as when someone is barking orders—how wrong this is! Christ taught His disciples not only what they were to do, but how they were to do it, as is seen in 1 Corinthians 14:35. For someone to show how something needs to be done, it requires that person to be an actual example. This is evident in Philippians 4:9. Unfortunately, it is quite easy to desire to be a leader without combining with it the recognition of the responsibility of being a servant who is consistently present with those he leads.

Finally, leadership requires one making *informed and correct decisions*, as well as *delegating responsibilities*. This requires the leader to secure the best person for a specified task. This is demonstrated in passages such as John 4:1; Mark 1:35–38; 6:7, and 6:35–43. Making correct, careful, and considerate decisions will certainly go a long way in being the right type of leader.

LOVE: Another aspect of being a leader is being *one who loves*. This dimension of love refers to that of agape love, which is the love that gives because of an awareness of need, and not because of the worthiness of the other person. Christ loved us with agape love. He saw we had a need and He chose to willingly meet that need. He did not consider what He was going to receive in return; instead He considered that He was able to provide the ones that were in need. The agape love spoken of here is, of course, found in John 3:16 where it is written: "God so loved the world that He gave ..." In this unmerited love, freely given, He took no thought of what He would get back.

In this aspect of loving, it is important to consider all facets of this word. The first dynamic is that of showing love in the area of the physical and the tangible. This refers to ensuring that there is *provision and protection*. There is nothing in the Bible to state that a husband as leader should have much by way of worldly goods and be able to provide extensively in the realm of monetary and worldly possessions. But what is required is that he takes care of his family. God's Word even says if a man does not care for his family he is worse than an infidel. (See 1 Timothy 5:8—"But if anyone does not provide for his relatives, and especially for members of his household, he has denied the faith and is worse than an unbeliever.")

A second aspect of loving involves the emotional state. This refers to a man extending to his wife and family his *approval and affection*. They need to know he loves them, and—as Christ died for us—that the husband would be willing to lay down his life for them. That offers such comfort and encouragement—the knowledge that their greatest needs will certainly be his greatest desires.

Loving will also require the aspect of *being a social companion*. Throughout marriage, it is extremely important that friendship continues to bring a couple back together again. That companionship reiterates, in an ongoing way, the importance of being physically present. You cannot be companions and be apart from each other. So, loving also necessitates helping in the area of *rest and recreation*. Recreation can be thought of as knowing what one needs to be refreshed. At times, a wife needs rest and time alone while at other times she needs to be able to enjoy a hobby to get away from her routine. A husband should be sure he meets her recreational needs and does not impose his recreational ideas on her, but sincerely helps in her areas of need.

Another very important aspect is that of *the sexual relationship*. God has directly said that the husband's body is not his own but is his wife's, and vice versa—see 1 Corinthians 7:2–5. Therefore, it is extremely important that the husband seeks to meet his wife's physical need.

And finally, it is important that he *meets her spiritual needs*. As a proper leader, he will look and note what the needs are and then come alongside and meet them. He will have to be sure to lead his wife in word and deed. It is easy to tell his wife that he will pray about her concerns, but much more care is revealed when the husband stops everything he is doing in order to specifically meet his wife's needs. He is revealing to her how this can and should be done. Ephesians 2:5–6, 1 Peter 3:7, and Proverbs 31:28 are helpful verses in this regard.

Words to women

The wife, from the beginning of time, was to complete her husband, but was not to be like her husband. God wanted man and woman to correspond to each other, not to be mirror images of each other. Therefore, the first role of the wife is that of submission.

Too often, people think of submission as if the one who submits is a slave, or one who is a doormat, reclusive and quiet. However, submission actually requires a great amount of energy and intensity. Proverbs 31 addresses the role of the virtuous woman. The woman in that chapter was not one who lay around and waited to be told what to do, but one who had her family's interests and husband's best interests at heart. She strove from early in the morning until late at night to meet her family's needs.

An important aspect of being submissive actually requires the wife to be willing to give her advice or opinions. In one sense, she should act as if she is the Executive Vice President of the marriage corporation that she and her husband are in. If she has the interests of her family at heart, then she will be willing to assist in the decisions that are made. The wife is in no way inferior, or holds an inferior position, to that of the man. Luke 2:51, 1 Corinthians 11:3, and 1 Corinthians 12 affirm that what is important is for her to realize that it is her responsibility to contribute to the family in this area. The man's position and the woman's position are different, but neither is inferior or superior to that of the other.

As mentioned, this will require effort on the wife's part. It does mean that it is the wife's responsibility to intentionally place herself under the leadership of her husband. Submission requires a lot of effort and sacrifice. However, knowing that she is commanded by God to be submissive, she realizes that, in following this course of action, she is obeying God. God has already stated that He blesses those who follow Him. Submission is mandatory and is a spiritual matter, and yet it happens easily and naturally when role relationships are exercised appropriately. It involves attitude as well as action and, in the end, both genders—men and women—have to realize that submission extends to all areas of life, and always specifically involving a yielding to God's authority. Scripture passages to support this include Ephesians

1:22, 5:22, 1 Peter 3:1, Luke 2:51, John 4:34; 14:15, and Colossians 3:18.

The wife, as was noticed early in Genesis, was also created to be a "help meet" (KJV rendering) to her husband. The wife was literally made to be a "help" (aid, help, support) and to be that "meet" (opposite part, other side—that is, corresponding to and fittingly right for— her husband). God wanted a woman to be man's help, to assist him to do better what He had commanded to be done. This is seen in 1 Corinthians 11:9. God made her to be a suitable helper, as shown, for instance, in Proverbs 18:22–31. As the woman was made as a helper corresponding to the man, it is important to realize that this was all by God's design. This does not cast her in the role of an inferior person but rather elevates her to the status of the church in relation to Christ.

She is a "help meet" and she fulfills many duties in the home. One of them is making her house into a home. She also needs to be dependable and trustworthy in managing her responsibilities. She can also demonstrate her great responsibility and needs by discussing problems, disagreements, thoughts and feelings with her husband in a loving manner. She should also be creative and industrious, keeping family goals as personal goals. By showing interest in her husband's difficulties and being willing to help him solve them, she reveals another way in which she can be a great asset to him. It is extremely important for her to desire to help in the establishment of the home by being all she can be to help meet the needs of her husband and family.

There are some related considerations to be mentioned here, and these include the following.

- It is extremely important that she help her husband in raising their children;
- It will be a great encouragement for her to be grateful to her husband;
- She should show confidence in her husband and demonstrate her admiration for him;
- She needs to maintain a good spiritual life.

Submission is never easy. It is difficult to place oneself under the authority of another person. However by doing so, the wife is following the pattern and command that God has given for there to be a home that honors Him and assists in the overall promoting of the gospel through a man and wife modeling, and thus demonstrating, the relationship between Christ and the church.

Communication—A gift that must be cultivated

A second extremely important area in marriage, and one that can cure conflict, is that of communication. Using Ephesians 4:15 as the premise, spouses should speak to each other with openness and honesty. However, it is extremely important that they speak the truth in love. It is not often difficult for people to speak the truth, but what is often difficult is telling the truth in love. It is when people speak the truth without love that the conflict and hurt begins.

There are three components to communication. Put this way, you should consider *what was said, how it was said,* and *how you looked when you said it.* Communication is transferring what you understand, know and feel into the understanding and feelings of the other person. It is important that all three components are considered when communicating something nicely. If you don't look at the person, this detracts tremendously from what you are actually saying. Similarly, saying something in a nice tone of voice, but then being distracted while saying it, diminishes the effect. That is why it is so important that people consider communication in terms of being "a gift."

Solomon speaks to this fact in Proverbs 25:11—"A word fitly spoken is like apples of gold in a setting of silver." Of all people, Solomon had everything at his disposal. On this occasion he may have received a gift that was so pleasing, he made the comment that a word that is fitly spoken is like this special gift he had received.

This shows how important it is to make sure that the words we extend are gifts that the other person would appreciate receiving. When it comes to choosing a gift for a loved one, we may go to great lengths considering what type of gift to give. We make sure we have the right color, size, and style so that the gift will be appreciated. If husbands and wives were to take that much time and evaluate the actual contents, tone of voice, and nonverbal cues in their communication, they would make great headway in this area.

While speaking to one another, it is extremely important to consider the following five guidelines:

1) Is what I am about to say really true?

2) Is what I'm about to say meant to help or hurt?

3) Is this the best time to say it?

4) Is this the best way of saying it?

5) Does what I'm going to say have God's direction— have I prayed about it before I say it?

If these guidelines were followed before every conversation, there would be very little that is wrong in our communication. Even if the information conveyed were not quite correct, at least the interaction would be such that it would be of great assistance. So, first of all, *spouses should speak to each other with openness and honesty.*

Secondly, *spouses should speak with self-control.* It is extremely important that spouses take the time to control their own emotions, desires and interests. They need to be most interested in their spouse in those specific areas. By controlling themselves, which of course involves their emotions and their overall nonverbal communication, they will do wonders in assuring their marriage partner that what they are saying is sincerely intended to help them. It will show, when they are maintaining self-control, that they are not about getting their way but about having it the right way.

A third aspect is that *spouses are to be patient as they practice good communication skills.* There are always times that a conversation begins on the right note and with the right intent, but, as emotions flare, the entire conversation becomes derailed. Spouses can become so embittered about the manner in which the conversation is going that they do not take the time to seriously listen to what is needed and what is being said. As spouses develop the grace of being patient, they should be careful not to get angry if the problem is not immediately resolved. They also need to make sure that they are humble and that they do not let pride get in the way if they are wrong. However, in all of this, the truth should never be compromised. If the truth is being stated in love, and if the guidelines expressed earlier are followed, truth can be articulated very easily and accepted very graciously.

In their communication, *spouses should aim to develop good listening skills.* In an electronic age, or in any age when people try to do more things than they really can concentrate on at one time, it is easy not to take time to listen. When you take the time to listen, be sure you let your husband speak without interruption. Allow him to completely state what he is are thinking and believing, even if you think you know what he is going to say. Make sure, as you are working on your listening skills, that you are giving your wife your undivided attention. Make sure there are no newspapers or electronic gadgets that are taking your attention from her. Make sure that when you listen, you listen with complete attention. Make sure that you accurately understand what she is saying or thinking. A great way to make sure of this is to actually repeat back to her, after the conversation, what she has just said. By repeating back to her what was just said, it confirms that you accurately understand. It will also solidify in her mind that she has what is necessary.

Finally, with listening skills, it is important *to look at the problem and the circumstance from the other person's point of view.* All spouses are great at knowing what they themselves think and believe. They are in complete agreement with themselves! But if they were to take the time to look at it from the other person's point of view, they would understand why there is so much difficulty in working through this.

Overcoming obstacles

There are some obstacles that can occur to good listening. One of them is *defensiveness*. At times, spouses may consider what is said to be an attack on their character or their ability, rather than understanding that their marriage partners are simply speaking the truth in love. The habits developed over time have, unfortunately, directed people to immediately think that something that is said that goes against their will is an attack on them.

A second obstacle is that of *preconceived ideas and responses*. You should be very careful that you are not already answering your wife or husband before the concern is completely expressed. Perhaps you have a clue or a good idea as to what the matter is, or you know what will be said—or how it will be said—but still it is important that you both work toward good listening and understanding, and take the right length of time to speak and listen properly.

Another obstacle is *interruptions*. At times it may be that your spouse interrupts before even hearing your entire statement. Your loved one must be willing to listen completely. When an interruption takes place, it is important for you both to realize that it is an obstacle and you must still work through it.

Timing is yet another hindrance to good listening. As some people are better at night and other people are better in the daytime, it is vital for you to find the best time in which to consider together the matters that have to be addressed when there are important decisions to be taken.

Finally, *physical exhaustion* can be a hindrance to listening. If you are starting to fall asleep or even if you are only yawning, it will rattle your spouse to the point where he or she will feel you are not even listening. Make sure that some of these obstacles are being considered in advance, and, if difficulties begin to occur, simply suggest that you should both discuss these at a time when these difficulties will not be there. One final rule is to make sure when you listen, you really are listening— with your eyes, ears, and body.

Three things specially to keep in mind

Even though obstacles may be considered, and even though you endeavor to avoid them, there are some problems that all people face in communication.

The first is that *we are all sinfully and deceitfully arrogant and selfish.* Our hearts are "deceitful above all things, and desperately sick," (See Jeremiah 17:9) and, because of that, it will be difficult to want to hear something from another person's perspective.

Another problem in communication is *there is a basic difference with the way men and women think and express themselves.* There is nothing wrong with that. In fact, God created men and women uniquely different from one another, and He said it was good. This difference, however, means that both people have to work to overcome the ensuing communication problems. They need to be sure to hear what is being stated, and understand it from the other person's perspective.

Finally, *there is a natural apathy toward dealing with problems* and instead, to accept the status quo. Not addressing something may initially seem like a great idea; however if you keep on not addressing it, it will slowly develop and become a major issue. That apathy will eventually result in a catastrophe.

Troubleshooting with gentleness

Since we know there will be obstacles to good listening, and that there will be problems in communication, it is important to address the method of overcoming these problems. First, it is extremely important for you to identify, confess, and then forsake the sin of their antagonistic communication with your marriage partner. Identify what the problem is, confess that problem, forgive that problem, and then forsake that problem.

It will be helpful to also recognize that each spouse has a part of the problem. It may be that your spouse has a higher percentage of fault; nonetheless, you both have some ownership in the issue. If you would both admit to your part of the problem, you will, in turn, be able to begin becoming part of the solution.

As couples begin practicing right communication, it will be extremely important to remember the following:

- *Discuss the present problem* with those who are part of the problem or who are part of the solution, and not with anyone else. Too often the people who most need to be in the conversation are the last ones to hear about it. Discussing the problem with people who cannot solve it only adds to the frustration.
- *Deal with the present problem* and not with the past. This book will address forgiveness in Chapter 8. If forgiveness is actually sought and extended, it means that the issue is no longer an issue. If you deal only with the present problem, because all the ones in the past have been forgiven, then you will stay right on track.

- There will be times when several problems will surface simultaneously. If that happens, *deal with one problem at a time*. Don't confuse the issue and try to make the other person look bad or feel bad. The purpose of your communication, and overcoming these problems, is that you have an intimate relationship. The goal is not to win by arriving at your goal; the goal is to win by giving in, or making sure the other person's point of view is considered and adhered to.

There also will be times that you may need to compromise. This is likely when you are facing an issue that is not addressed directly or indirectly by the Bible, or when it is essentially a non-moral issue. Some people squeeze the tube of toothpaste in a certain way; others rotate the toilet paper in different directions. There is absolutely nothing wrong with that—but it is amazing how many people will let that become a source of conflict. Angry conversations revert back to those little, trivial difficulties.

Be careful that you do not use emotionally charged words. Using words such as "never" or "always" are usually simply not true and create problems. After the discussion is finally concluded, and if for some reason no agreement is reached, then the husband, as the head of the home, should make a careful, correct, and considerate decision, and the wife is to abide by that. If the husband—as the head of the home—seriously wants to be the servant to those he leads, he will want to be sure that his decisions are made appropriately. Of course, there will be times that the wife will have an idea that she would like to present—and there is nothing wrong for her to share her opinions and beliefs, as was said earlier under the area of submission. However, she is to share that on a one-time basis. Once it is shared, then it is for the husband to take the final decision. This one-time sharing, used as an appeal, is wonderful. However, if it is continually brought back up because the spouse has not agreed to implement it, there is the danger that it may become nagging and it will then lead to a very difficult situation.

THE PHYSICAL RELATIONSHIP—A GIFT TO EACH OTHER

A very important aspect of the marriage is that of the physical relationship. If poor communication heads the list of marital complaints, the one-flesh relationship runs a close second. The romantic story in The Song of Solomon reveals that God has ordained the physical relationship for procreation, pleasure, and purity.

Sexual happiness in marriage will not occur naturally—as if just automatically—or by accident. It is, of course, an aspect of the relationship that, prior to being married, has been much anticipated by both the man and the woman. Unfortunately, our society today has tainted this beautiful gift that God has created for husbands and wives to enjoy. It has perverted it so that people become way too desirous of the physical act for pleasure alone, failing to realize the blessed union it creates and promotes in marriage.

In Scripture, God speaks specifically and directly of how special the physical relationship is and can be in a marriage. In fact, the Bible promotes the thought that it is imperative for the physical relationship to be the way it ought to be so that a husband or wife will not seek such anywhere else. Proverbs 27:7 speaks of how a full soul will loathe, or despise, the delicacy of a honeycomb. However, the hungry will literally eat anything—every bitter herb actually seems sweet to the hungry soul. Therefore, it is so important that the physical relationship be fulfilling to the point that neither spouse will ever want to be in a relationship outside of their marriage.

To develop the illustration from Proverbs 27:7, if you think of a dinner, you know what it's like to be full of your favorite meat and carbohydrate and vegetable, rounded off with a delicious dessert. For example, if you have a steak, baked potato, broccoli, and pecan pie, you will probably feel stuffed. So if you are asked if you would like seconds, you will look at that delicious steak that thirty minutes before you were ready to devour, and you will consider the delicious dessert that you couldn't wait to sink your teeth into, and say, "No, thanks, I am already full!" The same occurs in the physical union of a husband and wife. If the husband is so satisfied and filled with the "ravishing of the wife of his youth," and that she continually satisfies him, he will not look outside of his marriage. If her life is continually fulfilled in her affection and emotions because of the pleasure that continually occurs within the physical union, neither will she look outside of her marriage.

Couples should be committed to being used of God in meeting each other's needs. This relationship of the physical is essential in dealing with temptation; it powerfully heightens the partners' awareness of the unbreakable one-flesh bond that God has given them. God says in Hebrews 13:4 that the marriage bed is to be undefiled. A simple statement is this: "You may act married when you are married!" Within this very important area it is important to recognize that men and women are uniquely different in their desire for this. What is extremely important for couples to do here is—and I mean this quite literally—to set out and ask their spouse to write down a "wish list" of what he or she would love in all areas of the marriage union to occur within their marriage.

In this list, women will typically put down responses of affection, conversation, honesty, financial support, and family commitment. However, what's so important here is that these words are defined appropriately and according to that spouse. This is not the time to use a broad-brushed approach such as "All women like flowers; therefore I will give you a flower to make you feel that I'm being affectionate." That is just as converse as anyone saying that meat will satisfy every hunger need. It's not a one-size-fits-all situation but it can be that wives and husbands may list their specific desires or needs and then explain exactly what they mean by that.

Typically, men will desire sexual fulfillment, recreational companionship, an attractive spouse, domestic support, and admiration. Comparing the man's list to the woman's list reveals that they are in different categories. If the husband will take it upon himself to meet his wife's needs, and the wife will take upon herself to meet the husband's needs, the reciprocal relationship will be absolutely wonderful. He, by the very nature of giving to her, will do nothing more than have her desire to give to him, and vice versa. As he gives to her to meet her needs, she will want nothing more than to meet his. God reveals this; it is clear from His Word that we love him because He first loved us (see 1 John 4:19). The principle is that when one initiates appropriately, the other follows.

Therefore, in this one area, it is extremely important to recognize the value that you will receive by taking time to not only seek to meet your marriage partner's needs, but to make sure you identify them completely so you may meet them appropriately. In a marriage that is undefiled, the husband is deeply satisfied and the wife feels ravished as she was when she was first joined with her husband— and the stage is well set and ordained by God for both parties to enjoy this relationship which is intended for pleasure and mutual delight.

FINANCES—A GIFT FROM GOD

The matter of finances in the home can be a delicate one. At times, couples have waited a while before they get married and have become quite accustomed to independently having a bank account. They may have a long history of taking care of their needs by their own earnings. So therefore, in a sense, they have income that is personally theirs. However, when God ordains and blesses in a marriage, those words that are stated in the vow—"All my worldly goods I thee endow"—reveal that there is now no longer "his" and "hers" when it comes to money. It is from that point on that the "his" / "hers" dynamic ends.

The couple need to be sure that they are desirous of noting finances that are clearly identified as "theirs" and being sure that they are to be used for God's glory.

Finances are surely God's gifts entrusted to us. God gives us the ability to make money (Deuteronomy 8:18). He does expect man to do honest hard work. Therefore what we have ultimately belongs to Him, for the earth is the Lord's and everything in it (see Psalm 24:1.)

There are many things more valuable than money. God's point is that "... having food and raiment let us be therewith content" (1 Timothy 6:8, KJV). The Apostle Paul also says, "for I have learned, in whatsoever state I am, therewith to be content" (Philippians 4:11). So, contentment is not based on a dollar value but is based on knowing that God is in control and that He will take care of our needs.

Covetousness and discontentment about money is sin. A person who desires to have what is not necessary or in abundance out of greed, may be making that an idol, and God says that is improper. According to Proverbs 20:18, we must prayerfully plan how to spend the money with which God has entrusted to us.

For further guidelines on thinking through finances and working on realistic budgets, see the Finances section in Appendix B.

CHAPTER 8

Forgiving with "Intentional" Forgetfulness

12 Put on then, as God's chosen ones, holy and beloved, compassionate hearts, kindness, humility, meekness, and patience, 13 bearing with one another and, if one has a complaint against another, forgiving each other; as the Lord has forgiven you, so you also must forgive. 14 And above all these put on love, which binds everything together in perfect harmony. 15 And let the peace of Christ rule in your hearts, to which indeed you were called in one body. And be thankful. 16 Let the word of Christ dwell in you richly, teaching and admonishing one another in all wisdom, singing psalms and hymns and spiritual songs, with thankfulness in your hearts to God. 17 And whatever you do, in word or deed, do everything in the name of the Lord Jesus, giving thanks to God the Father through him.

Colossians 3:12–17

FORGIVENESS

Because all people live in (and have come from) a fallen condition, there are always going to be difficulties and misunderstandings in human relationships. So, in light of this, a very important aspect of any marriage relationship is being able to extend and receive forgiveness. There are several considerations to be kept in mind in this regard.

First, it is extremely important to realize that there is a need for forgiveness to be extended. As we see in Matthew 6:11–15; 18:22 f., and Mark 3:28–30, when sin is committed, it is necessary to seek forgiveness. When a person seeks forgiveness, it is necessary for forgiveness to be extended.

To truly extend and receive forgiveness properly, you have to realize what forgiveness actually means. Forgiveness is a promise not to remember another person's sins against you anymore. Forgiveness takes into account the fact that there was an offense. However it doesn't turn away from this, but deals with it. Instead of being upset and retaliating or ignoring the situation, you, as the offended person, realize that you must extend forgiveness. Forgiveness is granted in response to the other person's repentance.

Repentance is a change of heart, which means a rethinking of your relationship toward God, yourself, and your sin. It is restores the relationship between Christ and others. Confession is a personal recognition of guilt and liability and admission of this to God and any others who have been wronged. Forgiveness is necessary, but it can only be extended when the other person—the person who has committed the offense—seeks it. (In your heart, you can be prepared to forgive, and live accordingly, but it may be that you don't actually forgive until the other person requests it.) That can be difficult because, at times, one party—the person who has been offended—simply may not want to *extend* forgiveness, or perhaps the other party—the person who offended—does not want to *seek* forgiveness. During the times when the offending party does not desire to seek forgiveness, it is still necessary that the heart of the offended party be prepared to extend it whenever it is requested. Sometimes that can take the form of simply acknowledging a readiness to forgive, if and when the other person requests it.

At other times, it may help for the offended person to actually write a letter extending that forgiveness to a person who has not requested it. This letter is to be kept, in anticipation that it will be sent or given to the person who offended once he or she requests the forgiveness. Such tangible evidence can help and go a long way in assisting in acknowledging that the offended spouse's heart is prepared to show forgiveness.

The gift of forgiveness certainly costs the one giving it much more than it costs the one receiving it. But then, when you see the parallel in that—that Christ died on the cross so that He could extend the opportunity for us to accept forgiveness of our sins—you realize that the pattern has been established. Following Christ doesn't mean just acknowledging Him as your personal Savior, but it means patterning your decisions and actions on Him from that point on. Forgiveness is a godlike attribute, and is one that couples will need to become very familiar with and practice often if they are to keep the relationship as it ought to be kept. Once a couple recognizes that forgiveness must be requested and / or must be extended, it is also important that they consider what forgiveness really means. There are three points in particular for consideration:

First, when you extend forgiveness it means that you will not bring the matter up to the offending party again. That means you are not supposed to discuss it any further, remind your loved one of it, or in any way bring the matter up again.

Second, it also means that you won't bring up the matter with others. Unfortunately, it is so easy to talk about the failings of another person to other people. It is extremely important to recognize that once forgiveness is granted, no one else should ever hear about that offense again.

Finally, it is extremely important not to bring it up with the person that was offended. Once God forgave, He did not constantly highlight the sins that we committed and remind us of how great He was in forgiving us. He simply wants us to be able to understand and appreciate that forgiveness has been extended. He then promises to remove our sins as far as the east is from the west (see Psalm 103:12). He is not going to bring them up again.

God forgave my sin …

To assist in the aspect of forgiveness, you need to recognize what the basis of forgiveness really is. The shed blood of Christ is the basis of forgiveness. Jesus intentionally and actively lived a life of love and obedience to God, a life lived on behalf of sinful people such as we all are, with a view to dying as the Substitute for all who would trust in Him. The fact that He chose to intentionally forgive, notwithstanding our failings and inadequacies, reveals the fact that when we forgive, it is an active form of showing our likeness to Christ. God forgave us when we least deserved it and yet most needed it. Therefore, for you to be completely in submission to Him when you have been guilty of an offense reveals that you need that forgiveness, whether or not you deserve it. Patterning forgiveness after Christ's forgiveness will help couples to be all that they should be toward each other.

Once you have extended forgiveness, it is amazing what occurs in that relationship. For one thing, there will be less tension because the offense of the sin has been removed. Naturally, we realize that the person who did the offending is still a sinner and is going to continue to have the same tendencies to do wrong again. However, recognizing that fact helps you to realize that intentional forgiveness removes that barrier. Of course, the life of the offending party needs to change and needs to develop a new biblical response pattern, but the important thing is that forgiveness is now in place, and the person is properly forgiven.

And then, as in considering Ephesians 4:22, when forgiveness takes place, it is vital that the relationship with the forgiven person return entirely to normal. The principles of Matthew 18 are vitally important at this point. When you forgive, you really must be able to treat the other person—in action, thought, and word— without any hint of bitterness. Forgiveness has to be all-pervading!

Some tests of true forgiveness

It is then important to be able to test if one has forgiven. Here are several indications:

First, if you have been offended, can you thank God for the lessons learned during the pain? Romans 8:28 reveals to us that God can make all things work together for good to those who love Him and to those who are called according to His purpose. Thanking God will help you to realize that this was for your good rather than for your detriment.

A *second* test is for you, as the offended party, to see whether you can talk about the hurt without getting angry, without feeling resentful, and without the slightest thought the revenge. Ephesians 4:31 and Romans 12:19 note that forgiveness, and the extension of that, changes the entire dynamic of what a person is like. Forgiven people are able to be just like they were before the offense took place.

Third, if you have been offended, is there a willingness on your side to accept part of the blame for what happened? You will notice that if you will accept part ownership, like 1 John 3:18 and Titus 2:12 affirm, how you are able to assist in the process of change.

A *fourth* test to help people recognize that they have either forgiven, or that they really need to forgive, is if they can revisit the situation or people involved in the hurt without experiencing a negative reaction. The experience of being able to even let it come to mind and recognize that they have forgiven, solidifies the fact that they are in complete agreement with biblical instruction.

Finally, as God encourages us in Romans 14:19, Proverbs 18:24, and Romans 12:1, here is a question to think about: Can the offended party reward with good the person who has hurt him? The Bible's picture of heaping coals of fire upon somebody's head illustrates an extremely important aspect of forgiveness. This speaks to the illustration in Bible times when the family used coal to help with the fire in their house. The fire was necessary for heat and for cooking. When people ran out of coal, or their fire died, they needed to go get more coal to rekindle the fire. Being gracious to a person who had caused an offense—doing good to such a person and, as it were, generously giving more coal when it was needed—was a powerful way of showing significant grace in less than favorable circumstances.

Practical guidelines for culturing biblical forgiveness
There will be times when nothing seems to be working. The following is a series of practical guideline for working through some difficult issues. It may be that you won't want to get someone else involved right away.

First of all, each party, or the offended party, needs to develop a list of hurts. This might be called the offense list. However, the purpose of the offense list is to record and restore. The purpose of the offense list is not simply to enumerate the offenses to make the other person feel bad. The offense list is created because the person offended has already determined in his heart that, when he is asked for forgiveness, he is prepared to extend it. In all reality, he cannot actually extend it until it is requested, but he can be prepared to extend it.

Once the offense list has been created, and both parties are prepared to forgive, it is extremely important to come together with those lists and to work through this without emotional flare-ups. It is important, first of all, to let each party know what the rules of the sharing will be. The sharing is not meant for there to be a discussion, explanation, or even retaliation. The offense is brought to the other party and the response should be, "I am sorry," "I was wrong," "Will you forgive me?" This will assist in having a specific plan so that people realize that they are bringing these offenses to the forefront so that they can forgive and be restored.

Only after the offenses have been presented, and forgiveness has been extended, should each party come together with a prepared wish list. This wish list is quite simply the consideration of how they want the other party to be. In other words, write down either the expectations that at one time they had for their marriage, or discuss what they would like to see now in their spouse. Realizing that the one making the request is human, and the one they are seeking these requests from is human, will help them be sure they are realistic and attainable. However, God has specifically said that we can do all things through

Christ who strengthens us (see Philippians 4:13), therefore no matter what the expectations are, it is possible to do what is expected or requested. The purpose of the wish list is for one party to be able to express to the other what is desired.

Finally each party—each spouse—will then take the other person's wish list and endeavor to make that list his own "to do" list. By noting what his spouse wants him to be like, and by desiring to do all things to God's glory and for his spouse's good, he will take that wish list and seek to do all he can with it for God's glory. Using a "wish list" as a "to do list" will guide him in not being the type of husband that *he* thought he should be, but instead will guide him in helping him be the type of spouse that his marriage partner wishes him to be.

Of course, the majority of scriptural principles guide us on how we are to live before a holy and righteous God. Therefore, whatever the wish lists state has to conform with what God would be pleased with. At the same time, each spouse should realize that the other spouse—the one requesting certain changes in aspects of life—will help clarify the real issues and generate an understanding in practice of what needs to be done in the matter of esteeming the other as better than oneself. This can be wonderfully motivating in the process of progressive sanctification—becoming more and more like Jesus.

Using the previous simple suggestion—even if it is not easy to apply—will do wonders in helping a couple go from where they have been offended and are at odds with each other to where they can forgive and live and please and serve God by serving their spouse!

May God help you to do all you can to nurture and cherish your spouse so that your relationship is one that mirrors Christ and the church.

* * *

CONFERENCE-TABLE RULES

Seeing as most of the time couples do not have any other adults in the house except for themselves, they will need to have ways to discuss and solve conflicts which arise. There is nothing wrong with conflicts, but there is something wrong with *unresolved* conflicts. God says that we are not to go to bed angry (see Ephesians 4:26). Everyone needs to be forgiven and to have forgiveness extended before going to sleep at night. If this does not take place, the same unresolved issues will still be there the next morning.

The teaching of Ephesians 4 makes it clear that there will be times when there will be both discussions and disagreements. Rather than considering what we do "if" we have difficulties, we should consider what we do "when" we have those difficulties. A great way to do this is to find a designated location in your home that you will always go to in order to have these types of discussions. These types of discussions require certain rules. The rules for a discussion—in private, without a third-party—should be as follows. These are the conference-table rules.

First, both parties *must be honest*. In order for both parties to be honest, both parties must speak. They must speak the truth, and they must speak the truth lovingly. As was mentioned, in light of Scripture one must be willing to obey what God says rather than what man says. Too often our society directs people to get their own way. But God considers honesty to be more important than getting our own way. Also, God wants us to give others their way over our own. Doing right while speaking right serves to keep a person in close fellowship with God. Ephesians 4:15 and 25 urge us to make sure that we put away falsehood and speak the truth, and to be mindful that we do this lovingly.

The second important aspect of a conference-table is to make sure that you *keep current with the issues*. In essence, that means taking care of all grievances before going to bed. The purpose of keeping current is so that one is built up in love. If and when you wait to seek forgiveness over a difficulty, until the other party does the seeking, there will not be very much movement toward keeping current. Each spouse must be willing to state his or her concerns in love, as is mentioned in the first "rule," and then both should be sure to work through the entire difficulty.

The third important aspect of a conference table is to *attack the problem, not the person.* Ephesians 4:29 speaks to the fact that there should never be any corrupting talk coming out of a person's mouth. To not have corrupting talk means that only good should be spoken. This literally builds up the other person and should be fit for the occasion. It's not only supposed to build up but is also supposed to give grace to those who hear. Being mindful not to grieve the Holy Spirit will do wonders in directing how one speaks.

Finally, considering these conference table rules, *there needs to be an agreement to act and not to react.* It is so easy to want to get even, or to get your own way. You have to realize that you and your loved one must intentionally act and do right. As it is written in verse 31, you must let all bitterness, wrath, anger, clamor, and slander be put away from you. Moreover, you need to make sure that there is no malice. To do that, and to make sure that all of these are put away, the Bible's point is that there should be kindness shown to one another, tenderheartedness, and forgiveness of one another, as God in Christ forgave has forgiven His people. Verse 32 sums this up, showing how important it is to make sure that God and His word and His way are always kept to the forefront.

The Bible's emphasis on living at peace with all has to begin at home. God has given the framework for conflict resolution, and when you walk in—that is, when you keep in step with—the Holy Spirit, and when you implement practical steps such as the ones enumerated in this chapter, it is possible for you both to establish and maintain a happy and harmonious relationship in your marriage.

Appendix A

Honey, I'm Expecting a Baby!

3 Behold, children are a heritage from the LORD, the fruit of the womb a reward. 4 Like arrows in the hand of a warrior are the children of one's youth.

Psalm 127:3–4

PARENTING—A GIFT TO YOUR CHILDREN

While parenting may be considered a non-issue when it comes to marital intimacy and camaraderie, it can be a divisive area. One reason for this is that both spouses have been brought up in two separate and uniquely different environments. What their personal experience has been can often be considered the "correct" or "worst" way for child-rearing. Past experiences have their way of becoming present patterns. It is extremely important to discuss this area before having children and to be certain that you are both in agreement when it comes to parenting.

According to God's Word, parents are to bring their children up in the "nurture and admonition of the Lord" (see Ephesians 6:4). There are many specifics in how people are to love God and love others. The options that parents have "to train up a child in the way he should go" (Proverbs 22:6) are almost limitless, as long as what they are seeking to do is honor God with their parenting. God's desire for their children is for them to grow up serving and pleasing Him. That is why this can be such a challenging area for couples. Both will want to do what is right, but the means and manner in which they wish to accomplish this may be uniquely different.

By using God's Word as the resource for principles, and then applying this to a couples' family, they will be able to note and follow through with the joys and struggles that parenting affords. Without compromising standards, and without violating their own conscience, couples can look into God's Word, and recognize that "two cannot walk together unless they be agreed" (see Amos 3:3). The important part of parenting is that they should desire to please God in this area. Then they should make sure, along the way, that their relationship is what it is supposed to be, while doing so.

For a thorough and in-depth consideration of biblical parenting, see the author's book, *It's Apparent … You're a Parent.*

Appendix B

Practical Stuff—Quantifying and Calibrating

Download and print these pages by visiting www.itsapparent.org or scan the QR code below:

Enriching your marriage

The following material has been prepared as a series of appendix checklists and is intended to guide you in your own checkup. You may or may not want to write your answers in the spaces provided. This kind of self check may be something you could consider pursuing periodically throughout your marriage.

Marriage is a gift from God and we are a gift to one another. How much do you treasure your gift? How valuable are you as a gift to your spouse?

You are gifted for marital intimacy. God created men and women for intimate marriages. Marital intimacy is a oneness—a closeness, communion or unity—between a man and a woman who have committed themselves to each other until death parts them.

BACKGROUND INTRODUCTORY WORKSHEET (1)

Marital intimacy will be established in a Christian marriage as the couple follows God's model for intimacy. Reflect on your marriage and then:

Write down two significant events in your marriage:

1._____

2._____

List two words you would use to describe yourself:

1._____

2._____

List two words you would use to describe your spouse:

1._____

2._____

Suggest two reasons why you married your spouse:

1._____

2._____

Mention two goals you would like to work on in your marriage:

1._____

2._____

List two expectations you had when you were first married:

1._____

2._____

Marital intimacy begins at a heightened level when a couple is first married. If couples do not diligently work at being and doing all they should, each stage in married life may bring further and unexpected challenges to the different levels of intimacy.

On our first date, we …

_____

_____

While dating, we had the most fun doing …

_____

_____

I was attracted to my mate by …

_____

_____

My spouse was attracted to me by …

_____

_____

Considering Some Details

When you were first married, you brought into your relationship many preconceived ideas and expectations. These were as a result of the influence of your parents' marriage or from your observations other married adults. You also had some dreams and hopes which you anticipated enjoying as your relationship matured. However, there are some expectations which are never fulfilled because they are not addressed or ever realized.

Consider the following itemized needs for men and women, and write your definition for each related term: (Be sure not to write any "textbook clichés," but honestly evaluate and list your personal definitions of these desires.)

As you define each category, according to your perspectives, be honest and specific, for you are writing your needs for the benefit of your spouse who will seek to meet these. If you are honest, and the needs are met, intimacy will be achieved or enriched.

As you define each category, according to your perspectives, be honest and specific, for you are writing your needs for the benefit of your spouse who will seek to meet these. If you are honest, and the needs are met, intimacy will be achieved or enriched.

Use the two separate worksheets for the following exercise.

INTIMACY: WORKSHEET FOR HUSBANDS (2A)

Sexual Fulfillment

_____

_____

_____

Recreational Companionship

_____

_____

_____

Attractive Spouse

_____

_____

_____

Domestic Support

_____

_____

_____

Admiration

_____

_____

_____

INTIMACY: WORKSHEET FOR WIVES (2B)

Affection

_____

_____

_____

Conversation

_____

_____

_____

Honesty/Openness

_____

_____

_____

Financial Support

_____

_____

_____

Family Commitment

_____

_____

_____

WORKSHEET: CONSIDERING OUR INTIMACY (3)

(Use two worksheets here, one each.)

Print an extra worksheet from www.itsapparent.org. Fill out this worksheet separately from your spouse. Consider the questions carefully, and personalize each response according to you how you perceive the situation. Once you have finalized your answer, discuss these responses with your spouse.

How you experience intimacy now

_____

_____

_____

When it comes to conversational intimacy, the way I see our relationship is …

- ❏ We say a lot but reveal little of our real selves.
- ❏ We reveal our real selves, but we don't say very much.
- ❏ We say a lot and reveal a lot of our real selves.
- ❏ We say little and reveal little of our real selves.

When it comes to sharing with you what I am really thinking, feeling, wanting, or not wanting …

- ❏ I keep it well hidden.
- ❏ I reveal as much as I feel safe to share.
- ❏ I am willing to be vulnerable to you.

Some ways I avoid intimacy when we are getting uncomfortably close are …

❑ I laugh or crack a joke.

❑ I shrug it off and act as if it doesn't matter.

❑ I act confused—like I don't know what is going on.

❑ I get angry or huffy because I am feeling vulnerable.

❑ I look angry so that you can't see into me too closely.

❑ I get overly talkative.

❑ I get analytical—hiding behind a wall of intellectualizing.

❑ I change the subject so I won't have to deal with it.

❑ I act strong, together, above-it-all.

❑ I don't avoid intimacy.

From the list above, some ways I see you avoid intimacy when we are getting close are:

_____

_____

_____

The reason I avoid intimacy in this way is:

_____

_____

_____

The effect of your avoiding intimacy in this way is:

_____

_____

_____

I would be willing to … (add words in the spaces below) in order to build intimacy.

_____

_____

_____

Romance is an important matter and not an easy term to define. It will be considered in more detail in the following worksheet. To get your thinking going, write your definition of romance:

HUSBAND: To me, romance is:

_____

_____

_____

WIFE: To me, romance is:

_____

_____

_____

Now, compare your definitions with each other!

Thinking about Romance

The term "romance" gives couples a lot of trouble. This is usually because both spouses are seeking to satisfy differing definitions. As a result, needs go unfulfilled in this respect. They are each in pursuit of something different, though they give it the same label. They believe their partner to be in agreement of the same definition while they are seeking to fulfill a different one altogether.

The term "romance" does not occur in the Bible, but the concept does. When God saw that Adam was alone, He chose to create another human being to occupy that emotional void. He decided to create a corresponder, someone suitable for him or a help meet—appropriate—for him (Genesis 2:18).

After God completed Eve's creation, Adam was both excited and satisfied (Genesis 2:23) as he was now whole and could feel complete.

Notice verse 24, as he was now to be one flesh, and should, therefore, find his oneness fulfilled in his married partner, and no one else.Complete the next worksheets, individually at first, and then comparing your responses. After your discussion, you may both need to change your answers.

ROMANCE EVALUATION:
WORKSHEET FOR THE WIFE (4A)

When it comes to romance in our relationship, the way I
see it is (check as many of the following as you consider
appropriate):

- ❑ Our life together is one long romantic "high."
- ❑ We are romantic now, but I think we are growing
  out of it.
- ❑ We have a romantic side to our relationship that
  we can turn on whenever we want.
- ❑ Maybe someday we will have time and energy
  for romance.
- ❑ Romance is for the young.
- ❑ We have a sensible, solid relationship. Who
  needs romance?
- ❑ We have more important things to do than think
  about romance.
- ❑ What is romance?
- ❑ Other (explain) _____
  _____

When it comes to romance:

- ❑ I am romantic while you are practical and
  realistic.
- ❑ I am practical and realistic while you are
  romantic.

❑ We each are romantic in our own way.

❑ Neither of us has a romantic bone in our body.

❑ Other (explain) _____

_____

What sometimes gets in the way of my being romantic with you is:

❑ I get too critical of you.

❑ You seem too critical of me.

❑ I carry too many resentments from the past.

❑ I am preoccupied with more practical concerns.

❑ I am afraid you will reject me or put me down if I get romantic.

❑ I need you to get romantic first; I respond rather than initiate.

❑ I don't believe that I am really special to you.

❑ Other (explain) _____

_____

Reflecting on the romance in our relationship, what I appreciate is:

_____

_____

_____

When it comes to romance, some ways I would like it to grow are:

_____

_____

_____

A romantic experience I would like us to have is:

_____

_____

_____

What I would like to do about the romantic experience is:

_____

_____

_____

ROMANCE EVALUATION:
WORKSHEET FOR THE HUSBAND (4B)

When it comes to romance in our relationship, the way I see it is (check as many of the following as you consider appropriate):

- ❑ Our life together is one long romantic "high."
- ❑ We are romantic now, but I think we are growing out of it.
- ❑ We have a romantic side to our relationship that we can turn on whenever we want.
- ❑ Maybe someday we will have time and energy for romance.
- ❑ Romance is for the young.
- ❑ We have a sensible, solid relationship. Who needs romance?
- ❑ We have more important things to do than think about romance.
- ❑ What is romance?
- ❑ Other (explain) _____
  _____

When it comes to romance:

- ❑ I am romantic while you are practical and realistic.
- ❑ I am practical and realistic while you are romantic.

❏ We each are romantic in our own way.

❏ Neither of us has a romantic bone in our body.

❏ Other (explain) _____

_____

What sometimes gets in the way of my being romantic with you is:

❏ I get too critical of you.

❏ You seem too critical of me.

❏ I carry too many resentments from the past.

❏ I am preoccupied with more practical concerns.

❏ I am afraid you will reject me or put me down if I get romantic.

❏ I need you to get romantic first; I respond rather than initiate.

❏ I don't believe that I am really special to you.

❏ Other (explain) _____

_____

Reflecting on the romance in our relationship, what I appreciate is:

_____

_____

_____

When it comes to romance, some ways I would like it to grow are:

_____

_____

_____

A romantic experience I would like us to have is:

_____

_____

_____

What I would like to do about the romantic experience is:

_____

_____

_____

WORKSHEET CHECKLIST (5A)
WAYS, AS A HUSBAND, TO EXPRESS
LOVE TO YOUR WIFE

- Function as the loving leader in your home.
- Frequently tell your wife "I love you."
- Lead family devotions regularly.
- Smile and be cheerful when coming home.
- Help your wife do the dishes.
- Care for the children so she has some free time.
- Do something fun at least once a week.
- Sit close to your wife.
- Write love notes or letters.
- Let her know you appreciate her.
- Seek to set a good example before the children.
- Talk about her favorably in front of the children.
- Brag about her good points.
- Maintain your own spiritual life.
- Make plans prayerfully and carefully.
- Ask her advice when you have problems or decisions.
- Have a realistic, biblical, positive attitude toward life.
- Follow her advice.
- Plan a mini-honeymoon.
- Buy gifts for her—have a "Happy Love Day."
- Remember anniversaries and other special events.

- Run errands for your wife cheerfully.
- Give your wife your undivided attention.
- Get up at night to take care of the children.
- Plan vacations and trips along with your wife.
- Keep yourself attractive and clean.
- Ask your wife to pray with you about something.
- Refuse to disagree with her in the presence of others.
- Refuse to compare her unfavorably with other people.
- Be polite and courteous as if you were dating.
- Be helpful when your wife is not feeling well.
- Be on time.
- Prepare breakfast and let her sleep in.
- Put the children to bed at night.
- Encourage your wife to pursue her interests.

WORKSHEET CHECKLIST (5B)
WAYS, AS A WIFE, TO EXPRESS LOVE
TO YOUR HUSBAND

- Greet him at the door when he comes home.
- Let him know you like to be with him.
- Be willing to talk to him about his concerns.
- Support him.
- Tease and flirt with him as if you were dating.
- Sit close to him.
- Hold his hand.
- Express your love in words or notes.
- Enthusiastically cooperate with him.
- Maintain your own spiritual life.
- Ask him for his advice.
- Be ready to leave the house at the appointed time.
- Thank him in creative ways for his attempts to please you.
- Buy gifts for him.
- Watch sporting events with him.
- Keep the house neat and clean.
- Cook creatively and faithfully.
- Have devotions with the family when he is not home.
- Maintain discipline with the children at all times.
- Be appreciative and cooperative.
- Offer constructive suggestions.

- Run errands cheerfully.
- Seek to complete, not to compete with him.
- Be honest with him.
- Be willing to see things from his point of view.
- Refuse to nag.
- Share your fears, concerns, joys, and failures.
- Refuse to disagree with him in the presence of others.
- Desire to keep your family memorabilia.
- Brag to others about your husband.
- Be in full agreement with your husband.
- Keep in touch with family and friends.
- Keep yourself attractive and clean.
- Invite other people in for dinner and fellowship.
- Be satisfied with your present standard of living.

BUDGETING WITH CARE (6)

Together with your spouse, consider the budget worksheet below. Suggest ways in which you may be better stewards of what God allows you to earn, and how you may be more generous to Him and to others as you disburse what He has entrusted to you.

Gross Income per Month _____

    Salary _____

    Interest/Dividends _____

    Other incomes _____

Less

    Tithe _____

    Tax _____

    Net Disposable Income _____

Total Expenses per Month _____

Housing   _____

      Mortgage/Rent   _____

      Utilities   _____

      Maintenance   _____

      Other   _____

Food   _____

Automobile   _____

      Payment   _____

      Maintenance   _____

      License/Taxes   _____

Insurances   _____

      Life   _____

      Medical   _____

Debts   _____

      Credit Cards   _____

      Loans/Notes   _____

Entertainment/Recreation   _____

      Vacation   _____

      Other   _____

Clothing   _____

Savings   _____

Medical Expenses _____

    Doctor _____

    Dentist _____

    Prescriptions _____

Miscellaneous _____

    Subscriptions _____

    Gifts _____

    Other _____

School/Tuition/Child Care _____

Investments _____

TOTAL EXPENSES _____

Income versus Expenses

    Net Spendable Income _____

    Less Expenses _____

    Surplus/Deficit _____

Also available

IT'S APPARENT ... YOU'RE A PARENT!

Raising Godly Children in Today's World

John Lehman

128pp hardcover
ISBN 978-0-9899532-0-7

128pp paperback
ISBN 978-0-9899532-1-4

I'm a parent ... Wow! How should I best navigate through the wonderful, new challenges and opportunities that are coming my way? What wisdom may be gleaned from the Bible, God's living Word? Will God really enable the process to turn out well?
In six helpful, easy-to-read chapters, John Lehman, a family pastor and himself a parent and grandparent of several children, writes with passion and clarity on the great issues of bringing up children. Here you may read about topics such as

- Getting ready to become a mom or dad
- Preparing an overarching goal for your child
- Demonstrating what it means to live in submission to the one, true God
- Facing the consequences God has directed when there is disobedience
- Cultivating a godly parental model that emphasizes practical godliness
- Navigating wisely through the ages and stages that lead to adulthood

Rich in biblical content, this book will help steer you carefully through the many situations that come the way of all parents.
Read a sample chapter online at www.itsapparent.org.